C0-ASI-602

HOW FULL
THE
RIVER

by

Omar Eby

HERALD PRESS, SCOTTDALE, PENNSYLVANIA

HOW FULL THE RIVER

HOW FULL THE RIVER is the story of Americans teaching in Africa. The characters in this story are simply a composite of personalities and experiences. The book is based on fact; all experiences, situations, anecdotes, and descriptions are more than mere imagination.

This story shows all the foibles of the human experience when one is put in a new and strange situatiion. How do you deal with a British headmaster who thinks Britain still rules Africa? How do you come to a personal relationship with some African woman, and when you do, how do you raise your baby boy when he suddenly has ten very interested grandmothers to help?

HOW FULL THE RIVER is a no-nonsense, unvarnished view of a foreigner's life in Africa. The American teacher in Africa has the old forms of security threatened: his patterns of life, his position among men, and his past relationship with others. God replaces this form of security with Himself. As one teacher summed it up, "Without commitment to Christ, we are only ourselves."

OTHER TITLES BY THE AUTHOR

The Sons of Adam
A House in Hue
A Whisper in a Dry Land
Sense and Incense

HOW FULL THE RIVER
Copyright © 1972 by Herald Press, Scottdale, Pa. 15683
Library of Congress Catalog Card Number: 70-181578
International Standard Book Number: 0-8361-1617-8
Printed in the United States

*"No matter how full the river,
it still wants to grow."*

An African proverb

PREFACE

Jonathan and Evelyn Hiebert and Livingstone Teachers College, to my knowledge, do not exist. The Hieberts are a composite of personalities and experiences of teachers in the Mennonite Central Committee's Teachers Abroad Program in Africa — or TAP, as it is more commonly known. The same is true for the college, a composite of institutions in which TAP volunteers teach, though probably somewhere in Africa a school does exist by that name, in memory to the great missionary-explorer. So much for fiction.

All else in the book is based on facts. No experience, situation, anecdote, or description related is solely the product of the imagination. All accounts can be documented from the files of monthly reports, retreat report, letters, news items, and feature articles of TAP-ers sent to the MCC TAP office. TAP orientation materials and private conversations with former TAP volunteers were helpful in providing the authentic detail. I might also add that I spent four years teaching in Africa, from which certain impressions, incidents, and characters are drawn.

While no particular African country is named as the setting for Livingstone, the milieu perhaps best fits Central and East Africa. However, I have taken a few liberties with geography and climate.

It must be noted that in those African countries, such as Tanzania, which are pursuing an African brand of socialism, the educational and social life changes so rapidly for TAP teachers that their experiences do not fully approximate those in other African countries. Thus, what is written about a "typical" African teaching situation adequately described Tanzania, for example, a few years ago, but hardly does justice now.

While hundreds of TAP teachers made the book possible, I want to give credit to a few in particular, for their assistance in providing me with clearer insights into the educational and social life of Africa. I refer to Harold F. Miller, David Janzen, Phil Hofer, Judy Hilty, and Joseph C. Shenk, a Mennonite missionary. The TAP retreat account in chapter eight is adapted and condensed from a report by Eric Schiller. Thanks also are due to several former TAP teachers, for their critical reading of the manuscript: Ken and Kathy Neufeld, John and Barbara Mast, John and Lois Shenk, Ron and Gudrun Mathies, Lewis and Ann Naylor, and Ernest and Lois Hess, Mennonite missionary teachers. The chapter on the TAP wife was written by my wife, Anna Kathryn Eby; a special thanks to her. Finally, appreciation is expressed to Vern Preheim, MCC's director for Africa, under whom the TAP administration falls, and to Robert S. Kreider, the "father" of TAP, for their counsel and encouragements.

I am under no illusion that I have produced a book totally pleasing to every TAP teacher. I shall feel that I have succeeded if half the TAPers feel that the book accurately portrays their experiences — half the time.

Omar Eby
Lancaster, Pennsylvania

CONTENTS

1. FIRST DAYS:
Romanticism to Pragmatism

They took us in a little Roho, Evelyn and me, with the missionary driving, to a village church beyond the far hills east of the school. We had planned to leave that morning to attend the first session of the two-day Christian life conference. But a water pipe running from the tanks on the hill to the staff houses broke at a juncture, and water was soaking away in a great wet patch. Besides baptizing African believers, the missionary's other aquatic chore included the maintenance of the school's water pumps.

"Jonathan," he said to me wearily, "I'm gonna have to fix this bloody break before we can push off."

It took him and two African assistants the whole morning to repair the leak. So it wasn't until early afternoon that we were able to get away, and by then the sun was throbbing overhead and smiting the roof of the car. Along with the fine red dust, one smelled rather than actually saw, sifting in through the open car windows were great puffs from the hot afternoon.

I had been having some stomach trouble for the past two days -- the African male nurse assigned to our school thought it might be a touch of malaria or because of too much guava sauce. He couldn't be sure, just yet, he said, and preferred to

9

treat me for both, just in case. I would have felt no uneasiness had I been more confident of the nurse's diagnosis. For he wasn't really a fully trained and registered nurse, but something like a practical nurse, a "dresser" they sometimes called his kind in Africa. I suppose it meant that he was trained in dressing wounds, possibly those of leprosy patients.

That knowledge did nothing to quiet the strange shooting pains that started up midmorning, nor did the uncertain waiting around and trying to assist the missionary-plumber, who kept yelling for something called a spanner, and giving orders to hold this end and prop that bloody piece with this and run up to the go-down, the two African assistants and I falling over each other in an obsequious ballet of obedience. My having come from a long line of preachers and teachers and wives and mothers of the same did not prepare me for that moment, nor did the singular pursuit of Elizabethan sonnets.

As we jounced along the dirt road, swerving to avoid potholes and stray cows, the tarmac long since behind us, the shooting pains were reinforced by a steady grinding ache high in the dome of my stomach -- at least what I thought to be the dome. I would have said something to Evelyn, sitting thickly beside me, her face slid into a silly droop from the stuporous heat. But she had given me little consolation when earlier I had compared it to something like birth pains. She would not have that exclusive agony cheapened by comparison to a small grind in my gut.

The church sat on the edge of the village in what might someday become a suburb, should the village ever rouse its lethargic self from post-independence slumber, discover some natural resource nearby to help it break out of its doldrums of poverty, and grow. The missionary thrust his little Roho into the sketchy shade of a copse of thorn trees, and we limped out into the midafternoon quivering glare to join the brethren at their "new life" conference. The staid burnt brick church wore an incongruous outer frill, a floppy banana leaf-covered lean-to, underwhich the overflow crowd sat protected from the sun.

The afternoon session was already in progress, for a great voice, lifted in the vernacular, rolled to us through the open archways of the church. Our arrival stole the attention of audience from the speaker, though we tried to slip under the banana canopy as inconspicuously as four white people could at a predominantly African meeting. To master the situation, the speaker capitalized on our arrival and bawled to us a generous greeting in the Lord's name and demanded that someone at the rear door show us into the church. Evelyn and I followed obediently behind the missionary and his wife into the packed congregation, sweating but jubilant. My mind drifted back to the open air outside and the cool shade under the banana canopy. But staying there, more pleasant as it was, would have been an offense to the speaker's generous gesture.

He resumed his sermon with renewed turgidity, and as it was in the vernacular, of which I understood little, I spent the time concentrating on the language to isolate one word in a thousand, or in personal meditation. The afternoon wore on by the hour and the heat from so many bodies tightly packed overwhelmed me. The mind went limp with fatigue, concentrating on unfamiliar sounds or in private reflection. What Evelyn was doing to entertain or instruct herself spiritually, I do not know, but I found that shortly into the second hour I was contemplating the bat population inhabiting the rafters of the sanctuary.

During that afternoon, reality smashed through the imaginary, and for me the idealism of the first days in Africa slowly dissolved before the harsh light of realism. While sitting there on one of those low, backless, cement benches, designed with so little respect for human anatomy, I was thinking, chin thrust into my hands, elbows digging into my knees, and stomach grinding with sharp pains shooting up -- I was thinking about the whole situation I found myself in: the broken water pipe resulting in the delayed trip; this "new life" conference carried on solely in the local dialect and the missionary assuring us that many Europeans might be there and there would need to be a translation, and I not understanding a word and not getting any new life; the gritty cement bench under me staining the perspiring seat of my trousers; the cavernous, cockroach-infested house that I had brought my sweet wife to for three years; the surprisingly disrespectful students, giving one no reprieve from stateside teaching experiences; the endless days of my own mediocre teaching lying ahead. . . .

Evelyn and I left the prairies of the Midwest for the savannahs of Central Africa to teach in the Livingstone Teachers College for young African men and women. We had the Mennonite Central Committee's Teachers Abroad Program -- or TAP, as it is more commonly known -- to thank for "making us available to the world," as one of our fellow TAP-ers puts it.

TAP isn't an old program, only began in 1962. It's an example of the imaginative type of frontier programming MCC is known for, though up to the point of our personal involvement with TAP, MCC in our family, while a household word, was known as a tin of beef, a Christmas bundle, and a warm blanket for an Arab refugee -- aside from its Pax program, that is. But I've learned that MCC has a Voluntary Service program, a mental health service, that Mennonite Disaster Service is under its auspices, as well as a section for affairs related to peace and reconciliation. In the TAP program they have 200 teachers, a couple of doctors, a veterinarian, a librarian, and a nurse or two, in eight sub-Sahara African countries, and entered Bolivia and Jamaica as well. It was all very impressive, and as for Evelyn and me who had already taught a few years and taken care of our college debts, we were excited about the new venture.

From our commitment to Christ sprang a vision to serve our fellowmen. We had long observed that service was one of the best ways to communicate the essence of the Christian message to others. I felt that the Christian faces a world in which the encounters for communication or conflict are transcultural. If the Christian hopes to be a reconciling agent in times of crisis or simply a communicating agent at times of quest, he must himself learn what it means to have his life and faith shaped by a different culture. He must experience for himself the agony or ecstasy of communicating across cultural boundaries.

Thus, one of the reasons we selected TAP was that we felt it put us in contact with the culture and people of Africa, a new venture for us. We expected from the outstart that a rewarding and fulfilling experience would depend upon the personal relationships we would develop with our African associates, both teachers and students, and that also we could expect to savor on the tongue of experience that sweet taste of a mission being accomplished.

Admittedly, the motives for joining TAP might have been a mixed bag, but where is the Christian man or woman pure in his desire to serve? There was, I suppose, a little pride in me that said, if you serve in this matter, you will be an admirable example of the Christian servant motif. And just incidentally, you might also become great in the kingdom someday.

That hot afternoon in the village church, four

months after we had arrived in Africa, Evelyn and I began the humbling experience of facing reality.

All that had been picturesque became dirty; the quaint folk or custom, furious or stupid; the indigenous cuisine, insipid and glutinous; everything suddenly sounded wrong and smelled wrong. We wanted like crazy to get out of that brick oven of a church with its silly banana leaf verandah and go home -- home to the wide clean Midwest prairies, sweet under the sun, cool under the stars.

Even our calling did not escape its share of a clubbing by the truth. The missionary couple sitting next to me passed over an English New Testament, open to the African pastor's text. It was Matthew's account of Zebedee's sons' request to be honored by Jesus by being placed one on each side of Him. "Lord, make us great in Your kingdom," they were, in effect, asking. I looked up quickly, fearful that the words had actually leaped from my own mouth, for it was in truth what I had been yearning for unconsciously.

Most unexpectedly, I was receiving a "new life" word at the conference after all.

In the years since, I have observed that most expatriates in Africa go through a turbulent period of adjustment, usually about four to six months after arrival, when the negative side outweighs the positive. It has nothing to do with climate or diet or strange creeping things in their houses at night. It is not physical in any sense. Rather, I suppose, it is psychological and is concerned with relationships to a new people, and to their sense of values, and their patterns of thought and behavior.

The counselors and directors at TAP retreat label it "culture shock." How hard it hits often depends on how false the motives and how romantic the expectation. But there is some reassurance in knowing that all get hit with it. Some seem never to achieve a satisfactory balance, but spend the remainder of their time bitterly counting the days till their term is up. But for the most, who sustain the cultural clubbing and bounce up on the other side of purgatory, their stay becomes a delight to everyone. If anyone thinks that it is going to be picturesque, or if his sole equipment is simply a spirit of adventure and idealism, he should forget it. For unless he definitely feels and knows that this is his chosen field of work, that he has some concrete skill of hand or mind, and some gift of the Spirit to offer, TAP in Africa is not a place for him. At least that is the way it looked to Evelyn and me at the end of three years at Livingstone Teachers College.

The school sprawled up the side of a low hill, from which one could see the town four miles away huddled on the wide sweep of savannah stretching away to the eastern hills. It was such a beautiful place, when the rains came again in November and the land sprang up green, that it took one's breath in the early morning when one looked out over the plains to the mist-shrouded hills, purple and brooding. To the west, light would pour across the small fertile fields of maize, bananas, cotton, and cassava, and one imagined that the peasant with his short-handled hoe on shoulder was swinging along on a hard-packed dirt path to his shamba.

During the dry season, when the land lay panting like an old dog in a pool of dust, there was little life in the region, except for the bonfires which the herdsmen set to burn off the harsh dead grass so that tender blades would shoot up in the time of rains. It was illegal, this scorching destruction of the grassland, for the regional commissioner and the government's agriculture agent attached to his office said that it was. But nobody minded, and controlled flames continued to burn vast areas north of us each of the three dry seasons we were at Livingstone.

The heart of the town was the open market, though the small railway station ran a close second twice a week when the modern diesel train paused briefly on its east or west run over a single-track. It was the market, however, where we found everything under the sun, and from all parts of the world.

Like typical Europeans, Evelyn and I at first found many things which offended our Western sense of hygiene and aesthetics. But gradually as we strolled among the whitewashed stalls and learned to barter over the cabbages and three-corner heaps of tomatoes, we began enjoying our weekly market visit. The market food was cheap, the people friendly, and the situation offered no end of surprises. Suddenly, we might happen upon a tailor setting up his business right under a tree close by a woman selling her handwoven straw mats, and further on an open-air, itinerant barber next to a barefoot youngster guarding a great yellow mound of oranges and mangoes.

Between the market and the railway station one could pass along the main street, broad and open in the sun, shaded only by an occasional mimosa or flame tree. There Barclay's Bank held a key position, near the town square, as did the Anglican mini-cathedral, the Bata shoe shop, and an Indian Sikh's emporium. Were we to take a back street, we would find it narrow and its open sewers assaulting our delicate noses. Mule-drawn carts, bicyclists, playing children, heaps of refuse, an occasional Peugeot, and long-robed, turbaned figures of austerity shared the street with the brown, copper, and black-skinned Africans. Little shops were thrown open on to the streets, spilling their merchandise into the walkways so that one must step around them carefully. Under the verandahs by the doorways to their shops, the tailors had set up their treadle Singers, and stretched out bolts of khaki for cutting out some-body's pair of shorts, and some boy with a char-coal iron was pressing a brilliant blue smock on a packing crate -- all on the municipal sidewalk.

"Independence" is everywhere, these eight years after the country has gone through the trauma of cutting itself off from its colonial power. One can get "independence style" haircuts, eat "Independence Bread" or drink "Independence Beer," ride in an "Independence Taxi" on "Independence Road" to an "Independence Mennonite Church." The much-used phrase is becoming an old coin, so smooth-worn that it is losing its value.

The sight of hundreds of school-age children roaming the streets and marketplaces of the villages and small towns was one of the first things to strike a newcomer, especially if he was a teacher.

I could not help but ask, "Why are these children not in school?"

"There are not enough schools," was the answer, of course.

I knew this, and could even cite facts -- that only 60 percent of the nation's primary-age children can go to school, and only 19 percent of grade seven leavers can get a place in the secondary schools or teacher training colleges. To see the fact literally made the truth harder to absorb than to read about it. What future did such children have, I wondered, and what could they possibly contribute to their developing nation? Were such tremendous amounts of potential human resources, which the country needed so badly, to be wasted? There were to be no kind or easy answers for such questions, I was to learn.

In the nation's big city, the capital, one is struck by the modernity of architecture and transportation. The jet airport, built with an eye for the future, could handle the 747 Jumbo Jet with little noticeable crunch on the ground facilities. Luxury hotels of polished steel and poured concrete and plate glass rise a dozen stories above the city's skyline. Semi-trailers zoom over paved roads; Mercedes and Fiats flash along bougainvillaea-lined boulevards; the African secretaries mince out of their offices at lunch wearing mini-skirts.

Diversity is the hallmark of the African countries. Humble villages squat in the shadow of modern cities. One man lives in a modern cottage in a suburb while his brother inhabits a grass-roofed mud hut. High fashion and near rags pass each other on sidewalks. Yet because of this diversity, one can hardly escape the temptation to feel that some-where here, as in North America, there is a mis-placed sense of values and perhaps a misappropria-tion of funds. While urban life and rural life in Africa are as different as the twentieth century is from the seventeenth, yet they seem to coexist simultaneously there.

Television is a good example. Its presence in Africa was a surprise from which I never recovered. Granted, while the capital has the only telecasting station, and programming is limited to about five hours each evening, the few people who can af-ford acquiring a TV set make the whole proposi-tion less than convincing. Until small cheap receiving sets can be produced, so that the common villager can be reached, the TV station seems a luxury item for a developing nation.

But the radio is found in the most remote vil-lage, thanks to small batteries. All Africa is listening to the radio, to its own programs, whether they be in French from West Africa or Madagascar, or Radio South Africa, and to the BBC from London, and the Voice of America, as well as Radio Peking and Radio Moscow.

One soon gets into the habit himself — that is, if he is like Evelyn and me, who rarely used the radio in our home in the States. News we got by paper and TV, and could not stomach the wall-to-wall noise of the AM stations. But in Africa, the radio kept us in touch with the outside world. The blatant lies about the United States told over Radio Peking by a crisp, beautifully modulated English-speaking voice tempted us peace-loving Mennonites to become rabid nationalists and clamor for liquidating the yellow peril. Mostly we listened to the foreign programs broadcast by the European radios. Many played classical music by the hour in the evenings when reception was at its best.

It was by radio that we at Livingstone College first learned that our town was at last on the itinerary of the President's frequent air hops about the country. It was less than two months after Evelyn and I had arrived at our assignment.

"Jonathan, you're a lucky fellow," the senior TAP teacher said to me. "I've been here nearly three years and still haven't seen the President. Here you've barely arrived and are getting a chance fresh off." He said it kind of enviously.

We marched to town for the event in white shorts and white knee socks, something we teachers rarely wore, the white knee socks, I mean. Tan and green, yes, but not white. They smacked too much of colonial days and were a great bother to keep clean. The college band turned out in their purple and yellow costumes. The headmaster wore a felt hat for the occasion, so he would have something to remove in the President's presence, as a sign of respect, I suppose.

All the primary and secondary schools within walking distance turned out to greet the President, each with its own bands playing and school banner flying. The town emptied itself too, coming to stand in the newly cut grass at the small airfield, waiting to cheer their George Washington. The school bands had been stationed about the docking area at the end of the runway, and in the event the President decided to walk around the perimeter to greet the various schools on exhibit, the bands could strike up.

The dragonfly whirring on the horizon eventually metamorphosed into a small French-built plane which circled the town and lowered over our heads before setting down amid a cloud of red dust. It taxied to our end of the runway and stopped, wings spread before the excited crowd.

He came down the short flight of steps, waving and calling something to the people nearest him in the cheering crowd, who had to be held back severely by the police. He was a small man, more brown than black of skin, with a toothbrush moustache above flashing teeth.

The schools were not disappointed. He circled the crowd, lingering before each cluster of students

to read carefully the name on their banner. Livingstone College's men and women were placed beside
the boys and girls of a mission school. I shall not
soon forget the aesthetic jolt I got from the
juxtaposition of their band playing "Tell Me the
Story of Jesus," as their national President approached them. Fortunately he was educated in
Catholic schools, and I could only hope that he had
not learned the band's Protestant tune.

The incongruity of that situation was not unlike
another incident which happened on Livingstone
campus some weeks later. We were having a school
Sports Day when most of our 200 fellows and girls,
according to their dormitory teams, were challenging
each other before numerous visitors from town, the
wife of the town's mayor being among them. She
had been invited especially, to present the ribbons.

Midafternoon, during the heat of some athletic
contest, I noticed that three small herd-boys were
urging their forty-some cows on to the edge of the
ball field, so they could keep one eye on the shot
puts and high jumps and the other eye on their
black bulls and dappled cows. It was rather like
Menno Klaassen's sons bringing their registered
Holsteins to graze on the ball field at Central
High to watch a senior-junior tug-of-war during
a Field Day at which Mayor Daley's wife was attending -- except that our town was not so large
as Chicago.

Too soon, Evelyn and I found, such happenings
were apt to become commonplace to us so that we
had to arouse ourselves repeatedly to keep alert

to the more subtle and important difference Africa has in handling her own affairs. We wanted to keep our eyes open, for while we were teaching, there was much to be learning.

2. HEADMASTERS:

Capable but Threatened

"African countries have often assured American teachers of a welcome here that is genuine and undoubted," the headmaster of Livingstone Teachers College wrote to Evelyn and me while we were yet in the States.

Mr. G. B. Robertson -- or H/M, as he initialed his notices for the school bulletin board or memos to us teachers -- replied to our letter requesting detailed information about Livingstone. It was, what you might call, a courtesy letter, for we had a much more impartial source of information from another TAP couple fresh back in the States from Livingstone. They agreed to spend an afternoon with us at our apartment in Kansas en route to their home in southern California. It was they who urged that we write the letter.

"Just writing that letter to the headmaster will place you much higher in his view of rookie Yankee teachers," they said. "Once there was a teacher of his own mission studying language for two months in an adjacent country, but never wrote his head-master-to-be during that time. Mr. Robertson gave him a long time to work out his penance for that academic faux pas!"

The prompting added to an abstruse intuition we had that we ought to write the headmaster, when we learned from the Mennonite Central Committee exactly where we were being placed in Africa.

"Some Americans, however, feel anxiety in coming into an educational system that has been in the hands of the British for many years, and even though the country is independent, it is still very largely British in pattern. As an English headmaster, therefore, I want to reassure you.

"There has been some conflict in places, but you missionaries should not meet it in schools like ours."

Missionaries! The word leaped from the page to spear the eye. Missionaries? Not Evelyn and me. We didn't object to working with a mission in Africa, or perhaps to even being sent by our mission board, but please, kind sir, spare us the sun-helmeted image of that word. TAP-ers are just Christian teachers, not missionaries. Surely he knew that from the other TAP teachers working under him. Or was it his diplomatic way of underscoring certain spiritual qualities he expected in his staff?

"In the first place," he continued, "the only fixed standard set before us is the Christian one, and that is not the possession of any people, or mission agency and church, or continent. In the second place, we are not even trying to reproduce the British system. Examinations do still determine the curriculum to some extent but of the students going overseas for university studies, we have as many going to America as to Great Britain. Anyway, we are now helping to work out their own system in response to local needs. All we can do is to offer our experience and help in this creative task. It is less easy than imposing our own ideas but far more exciting. We are glad, therefore, that Americans are represented on our staffs. And if some American ideas and methods prove their superiority as they seem to be doing in mathematics teaching, for example, that is a gain for all. We are all learning as well as teaching."

During the August TAP orientation at the MCC headquarters in Akron, Pennsylvania, I read **Education for Self-Reliance**, by Julius K. Nyerere, president of Tanzania. Without discounting the education of an earlier era, its shortcomings were clearly stated.

"The education provided by the colonial governments in the two countries which now form Tanzania was not designed to prepare young people for the service of their own countries; instead, it was motivated by a desire to inculcate the values of the colonial society and to train individuals for the service of the colonial state," Nyerere writes. "In these countries the state's interest in education therefore stemmed from the need for local clerks and junior officials: on top of that, various religious groups were interested in spreading literacy and other education as part of their evangelical work."

I was delighted to learn that my headmaster's thinking so paralleled that of one of Africa's greatest realistic innovators.

Headmaster Robertson's letter went on to warn us that we should not think that we are just the same as the pupils. A mere casual acquaintance can do a lot of harm, he thought.

"In the first place the parents, as well as the political leaders, expect a strict standard of discipline to be displayed by everyone, including students, as the new nation emerges. The pupils are certainly keen to learn but do not always know what is best for them.

"Second, Africans have a culture and deeply respected customs of their own. In some ways, they are more mature than European young people their own age. They mistake too hearty a familiarity as rudeness or as an invasion of their privacy. Africans do have a privacy, personal and collective, though after you have been in the country some months you may doubt that, as you begin to feel that they are crowding you, an experience common to Europeans new in Africa. But it is more a matter of discerning what they consider private, and how this meshes or differs with the European's sense.

"Some Americans seem to spend most of their spare time among their own people. Others go to the other extreme and try to get close to the Africans by running down everything European. But we are aiming at building up in the country a nonracial community, and in the school itself a part of the Christian family.

"We have seen at this school members of your mission fitting in splendidly with these two ideals. Let us please have many more. The time is short and the task is urgent."

Headmasters are as diverse as human nature

and the teaching situation. Evelyn and I were grateful for every kindness Mr. Robertson showed us the first days we spent settling into Livingstone life, domestically and professionally. We were divinely spared the agonies we heard other TAP-ers relating at retreats. Some had headmasters who treated their staffs as they did the school boys, giving them tongue lashings publicly; others violated even a minimal code of professional ethics by passing along confidential staff matters to missionaries outside the school. Single male TAP-ers recounted with horror the loss of their dignity and manhood by having to beg for permission to leave the school for an overnight venture, whether for mountain climbing or bush church visiting.

My one complaint with staff matters at Livingstone, were I to have voiced it, would center on the inferior status new teachers endured. Having had a stateside satisfactory school situation in which I had earned seniority and respect of my colleagues was detrimental to my well-being at Livingstone, until I decided to forget the whole thing. The headmaster, unconsciously perhaps, conveyed the feeling that if you had not taught under him at Livingstone, you had not yet taught under anyone anywhere that mattered. Every other academic situation was inconsequential to Livingstone, thus the rookie teacher was a junior staff member, a person who was expected to perform and not question.

Occasionally we could not follow the headmaster's

logic in action or reaction. "It's the principle of the thing," he would exclaim indignantly at some new order handed down by the Ministry of Education which countered his own ideals. "It's the principle of the thing they are violating!"

Shortly after we were at Livingstone, a small episode took place which illustrated the headmaster's occasional departure from the rational.

A Mr. Peele, a fellow Englishman, as was the headmaster, but one who swore by the Royal Crown that he could not understand the "old boy," as he irreverently referred to the H/M in private, flew into our living room one Saturday afternoon distracted with frustration. He paced about the room, rummaging his hair and slapping fist into palm as we tried to compose him with a cup of tea.

"That man! That man! He's incredible! There are days when I swear the old bloke has gone right out of his head! Too much sun or equatorial water or malaria! He's mad, absolutely mad!" he cried.

"Have some tea, Peele," we said.

"Do you know what his latest bit of asinine nonsense is?"

"No? Shock us!" we cried.

"He's not going to let my drama club go to the capital to compete in the national dramatics contest. All that bloody work down the drain! He says that Livingstone was mistreated the last time we sent students up for meets in the capital, and that he has complained to the Ministry of

Education, and they have deliberately snubbed him by not replying, and now he is going to protest by not sending anyone to the dramatics contest! Can you imagine? A silent protest! A boycott! I ask you, who among all that great crowd in the capital is going to know that Livingstone is not present because we are protesting!"

We laughed -- at the absurdity of the boycott and at Peele's momentary derangement.

"Do you think he consulted me for my opinion? Indeed not. He probably thought it was sufficient that I simply be informed of his decision."

We sat about the room for some minutes commiserating with Peele. Having seen the drama club on the school's stage, I was secretly suspicious that the H/M might be keeping them home for other reasons. While they were good, the would-be dramatists, in my opinion, overacted every scene, so that the total effect was one of hamming it up or slapstick or sudsy bathos.

The next day we heard that the headmaster had rescinded his boycott against the bureaucrats in the capital and was allowing the drama club to enter the contest.

"He's mad, absolutely mad!" Peele muttered again on learning of it.

Midterm during our second year, Mr. Robertson decided to return to England, for the sake of his children's education. The Livingstone Board of Governors followed with their most enlightened step in years by appointing an African as headmaster.

31

During the next eighteen months, Livingstone Teachers College rose and fell with the glory and shame of the brief careers of three successive African headmasters. It was like a game of educated African musical chairs, played to the beat of an inner-drum, but everyone agreed that it was essential to have an African as the head of the college.

The Board of Governors called a Mr. Aristablus Minzimanonu to the headmastership. He had just returned from auditing theology classes in Sweden for three years, and it was his first administrative assignment. He was hard working, reserved, and in many ways a capable supervisor, but his lack of confidence caused him to be supersensitive. At least I judged him so because of his resistance to suggestions, especially if made by Europeans; he was extremely reluctant to allow the staff to help make decisions concerning school policy. Staff meetings were frustrating and not infrequently heated. Suddenly, one day late in October he announced to the staff and the Board of Governors that he had accepted the post as deputy secretary for political education. Within five days he left for the capital.

To fill in the gap, the governors next called home a Mr. Deusdedit Nyamuhokya, who was finishing up his doctor's degree in education at the University of New York. He proved to be a refreshing change, quickly transforming the staff into a decision-making body, and things began to happen. More changes took place during his six-month reign than during the previous two years we had been at Livingstone. New facilities for the school library were arranged, as well as dozens and dozens of new books purchased. A combined basketball-tennis court was built, and a track field laid out. Compulsory attendance at evening chapels was dropped, and the Student Christian Union promoted. Finally, a new general science laboratory was equipped.

Mr. Nyamuhokya, however, was anxious to finish his doctor's thesis and accepted a lectureship position at the national university; it agreed to give him a year and a half at full salary to finish his thesis if he first lectured at the university for two years. The Board of Governors and the leaders of his church were not happy about such attractive bait, and their appeals to higher motives were futile.

Nyamuhokya is one more African whose overseas university education had been paid for by his church, who had agreed to come back and serve his church for a specified number of years, and who then failed to honor such a commitment.

The African bishop and other leaders of the region had a dream. With financial help from the World Council of Churches and the Theological Education Fund and the Lutheran World Federation, and the Lord knows what else, these leaders wanted to educate their own men who could then replace the expatriate teachers at such places as Livingstone, and assume much of the administrative role of the numerous church offices. Their educated men were now returning with their master's and doctor's degrees smug under their arms, and the church in this region was learning, like so many others, that the men they had helped to educate were not coming back to serve the church. They were attracted to the capital, mostly, to high-paying prestige jobs.

The last African headmaster I taught under was Mr. Zephaniah Methuselah, who did not expect to be a headmaster at all, and by his actions and reactions seemed both delighted and frightened of his sudden eminence. He had only recently received his bachelor's degree from Cuttingham College in Liberia, Monrovia, West Africa, and was planning to be at Livingstone for only a few months before going on to Australia to do a master's or a doctor's or something. However, he agreed to fill in while the board searched for a permanent replacement.

Under Mr. Methuselah's administration, the college plunged into its first student riot, which was unfortunate for the headmaster's record, for the grievance had nothing to do with his leadership.

The hubbub started in the student mess hall at suppertime, and the headmaster and Mr. Peele, who happened yet to be in the staff room, went down to see what it was all about. It had to do with food, with the demand that their mush be made from flour of husked maize kernels, which was said to be sweeter, than the mush made from flour of whole-grain maize kernels, said to be bitter. How the headmaster and Peele found that out, amid the uproar of students standing on tables and throwing handfuls of the stiff mush about the hall and beating their enamel bowls on the table in protest, was surprising. Over his head a chant was taken up: "We want good food. We want good food! Good food . . . good food . . . good food . . ." washed back and forth between the walls and carried out the windows to the staff houses.

When the headmaster tried to quiet down the leaders of the protest in order to reason with them, someone shouted, "Kill the headmaster! He's a tight-fisted Scrooge!" In antiphonal response, the chant was raised: "Kill Scrooge! Kill Scrooge! Kill Scrooge!"

With that in his ears, the headmaster hurried to his house, snatched up his wife and five children, and dashed off in the school car for town, leaving the rest of us to face mockery and possible extermination.

Some ingenious fellows broke open the locked electrical boxes and threw the switches to the staff houses, plunging most of us at our dinner into darkness, but letting on their own school lights. Then the howling started, that demented human noise of man turning animal, and the crowd surged toward the headmaster's house.

Since our house sat off to the side, Evelyn and I could not distinguish the nature of the disturbance. So I started across campus toward the lighted staff room. Rocks whizzing past my head encouraged me to beat a hasty trot back to my house, thinking of my wife alone. We listened and watched at a window to hear loud cries for admittance at the headmaster's house, and when it was discovered that he was not home, fellows pitched rocks through the windows and smashed down his little banana shamba by the side of his house and snapped off a stand of young papaya trees.

Apparently remembering that their grievance was food, the mob doubled back on itself, returning to the kitchen and the storerooms, the cooks fleeing before them after making a few virtuous slashes in the air with meat cleavers. Students snatched up several bags of the hated flour and a couple bags of peanuts and sparked off one of the wildest peanut scrambles in the school's history of party amusements, with the corn flour drifting heavily into the grass and pathway before the dining hall, so that in the half-light of the fluorescent bulbs it looked as if Livingstone had been visited with a crippling hoarfrost as judgment for student devilry.

Into this scene drove two vehicles, the head-master's and the official car of the regional educational officer, whom Mr. Methuselah had gone to for aid. The abrupt flash of their car lights split open the scene and froze the rioters. The officials sprang from the vehicles without stopping their motors, and marched fearlessly into the frozen foray.

"I'll give you five minutes to get into your assigned classrooms for a roll call," the educational officer bawled to the students, waving his walking stick threatingly at their heads. "Anyone not in his room by then will be expelled!"

In the minute of absolute silence that followed,

someone tossed a rock at the officer, hitting him squarely on the forehead. His mouth flew open but he was so stunned that he could not cry. But the rock triggered the response among the rebellious group of students. They bent in the dark, scrambling for rocks.

The educational officer and the headmaster dashed to their awaiting cars and tore away into the night, rocks clunking on their car roofs, their tires spraying the bystanders with pebbles.

Only minutes later the Klaxon of a police car could be heard screaming toward the school in the night, and then they arrived, two police Land-Rovers careening onto the campus, their khaki-suited drivers popping out, billy clubs waving. Backed by the police, the headmaster regained his authority promptly, took a roll call and found seventeen missing, all fellows, thank goodness, I thought. While the girls screamed and beat their bowls on the tables, they had not entered into the rock-throwing melee.

The police took seven riot leaders with them to the lockup cooler for the night. Three of these were first-year students, which shows how well the selections were, I suppose. Later three students were expelled, one of whom was the son of an influential pastor who pressured to get the lad readmitted. It continued impossible to teach for the two days following, so great was the wake of the disturbance, with students even going around to the headmaster's house with their little cameras to photograph the damage, leering all the while, and being chased off by his wife with shouts of "animals." Eventually, flour of husked maize kernels was substituted, which seemed like a victory for the rioters, and conditions returned to normal.

It was rather like a miniature United Nations -- the Livingstone College staff -- with teachers from England and Scotland, the United States and Canada, Australia and New Zealand; we also had a socialist from East Germany, a black Rhodesian, and a white South African, and of course the national African teachers. Not only did customs differ among the staff, but also methods of teaching and the usage of the English language, the medium in which we all taught.

The British teachers' different sense of values made them, for the most part, apprehensive about everything American. Attempts at open discussions with them only seemed to result in the hardening of their opinions. Some of the American teachers from the self-acclaimed "faith missions" -- meaning they ventured into mission work with God only in faith and without the securities of denominational bureaucracy -- were equally as rigid, however. When I had differences with the other Mennonite teachers I voiced them, but with many of these "faith missions" teachers, it was unwise to probe, even gently, their motivation or rationale, or to ask questions to get them to discover their humanity; they were rarely open to a discussion of differences.

"My son went to the army to defend our country which allows you the freedom to be a conscientious objector!" one fellow American colleague snapped when it appeared that I was about to brush the subject of his church sanctioning military activity. I could almost have endured the tiring rejoinder, had he not said it so loudly in the staff room, looking about him solicitously to the other teachers, as though he had clinched the subject with a profoundly original argument. Such subjects were better left untouched, with certain of one's American colleagues.

When some disagreement arose with an African teacher, I soon observed that I always had to take the initiative to resolve it. I attributed it to the understandable excesses which the people of a newly independent nation might unconsciously display as they flexed their young muscles of freedom and prerogative. I certainly found it true, what one Mennonite missionary alerted me to watch for -- that an African will never refuse your confession. Between offended Americans, when the one is seeking to clear the air, the other will often say: "Please, just forget about it. I hold nothing against you," which, in itself, is often not true. In that sense, we Americans rarely allow each other the freedom to admit our error. But not the African. He will agree that "Yes, you were wrong." Or, as an African teacher replied once to me when I had gone to him to resolve some differences: "Yes, Mr. Hiebert, you have a hot stomach," referring to some anger I displayed at a certain stupidity I felt he possessed.

Yet, the African teachers, particularly Sospeter, were a great help to me during the first weeks of living and teaching at Livingstone. Sospeter and I were assigned as classmates to the first-year students. Unfortunately for him, my being new forced him to carry much of the load. He was also my mentor for discovering the school's unwritten policy on an endless number of subjects. When I arrived, the deputy headmaster gave me a booklet on "Rules and Regulations for Students at Livingstone Teachers College" which said little of value, except for the very end, where I found an illuminating sentence. "A new staff member is expected to get all the details from his colleagues." Not the headmaster, whom one might have thought to be the source for his orientation; thus, I was profoundly thankful for Sospeter.

Even so, the first month I would wake up about four o'clock in the morning and just lie there in the darkness and dread the day ahead, mostly the classes for which I had no training, particularly something called "Pedagogy," which was to teach the students how to teach. And African sociology, the absurdity of which my trying to teach it bordered on madness, for what did I know of Africa and her peoples to teach a year's course? So I would lie there sick with dread and throwing out little distress signals to the Divine, whom I felt led me into all this beauty, yes, and madness, until I began to chart a course.

We checked the library titles for subjects on

Africa, and then all the bibliographies of all the library titles, and wrote to all the ministries of the government even distantly related to African sociology, and also tried the embassies of the foreign governments for free booklets and pamphlets. Indeed, we'd take anything they'd mail us free, thank you. Until returns came from that lesson in letter writing, we invited in some of the chiefs from neighboring villages, asking them to explain the traditional forms of tribal government and recount the history of the region. We collected proverbs from the different tribes represented in the class and exchanged hunting and fishing tales, and swapped assorted stories which I labeled "National Folklore" to give the good fun in class an air of academic respectability.

The large classes — thirty-five students in each — and the lack of some basic equipment and supplies, even textbooks for such a class as the one in sociology, were the greatest hurdles for me to cope with. I suppose that reflects the educational affluence prevalent in middle-class American high schools in which I had taught earlier.

Livingstone had other peculiar distractions, too. One afternoon in the middle of discussing excerpts from the writings of some black Americans, we saw passing by the classroom a chief seated on a cheetah skin, carried by four porters. On another occasion, shortly after the rains came, and the tall grass had sprung up, a herdsman suddenly appeared on the campus with some fifty head of cattle. The principal sent the third-year fellows out to drive the cattle away, which angered the herdsman so that he began to run after some of the students, shouting and waving his long stick. Confusion reigned for some minutes both outside the classroom as well as within, until both the man and his cattle were gone.

Another characteristic of the classroom at Livingstone was to have students self-conscious about their role in shaping the destiny of their nation. During the early years following independence, the majority of the national assemblymen and civil servants, and other second-layer bureaucrats in the government, were little more than a black "colonial" government. Many having been trained by their colonial superiors, they unconsciously assumed the same mentality toward their positions and the nation's priorities.

A few years later, a realistic appraisal of independence was given, and the more insightful leaders discovered the meaning of their nation's own limited resources. Students were looked upon now as one of these resources, who no longer would be guaranteed a slot in the white-collar future. The purposes of studies must be redirected -- from merely passing certain examinations to serving the priorities of the nation. The student would have less and less options to choose his career and how and where he would practice it; the nation could not afford such a luxury to a segment of its society, and certainly not the trained brainpower segment.

Slowly the students struggled with reforming

their ambitions. The attempt to express these reeducated motives was occasionally self-conscious, as when they would try with mustered conviction to convince themselves and their skeptical class-mates that it was just as important for them to find their way back to their villages and invest their lives in the soil as it was to use their education as a first step toward a job in town.

This reformation in educational thinking –– a slow uncertain wind moving across the black African con-tinent –– is best expressed by the President of Tanzania, who wrote:

"Those who receive this privilege (education) have a duty to repay the sacrifice which others have made. They are like the man who has been given all the food available in a starving village in order that he might have strength to bring supplies back from a distant place. If he takes this food and does not bring help to his brethren, he is a traitor. Similarly, if any of the young men and women who are given an education by the people of this Republic adopt attitudes of superiority, or fail to use their knowledge to help the develop-ment of this country, then they are betraying our Union."

He could have been writing for all of black sub-Sahara Africa, so universal was the truth of the statement. At least during our years at Living-stone, the staff sought to inculcate that ideal: that one's gifts, his training and heritage, even his faith must be hammered into a bridge over which others could traffic. Selfishness only uses such en-

trustments and opportunities for personal en-
hancement, security, and comfort. It was not an
easy ideal to teach or to live.

3. STUDENTS:

Magnificent and Maddening

I went into TAP expecting difficult situations. But rarely did I find the climate, people, or living arrangements impossible. In fact, from May to August the weather was like a summertime on a high prairie in a Midwestern state: gently cool nights and wide sunny days. Then it got hotter and the cloudless sky glared like polished brass. But the November rains freshened the land and people again, and it was holiday weather for another six months. The people were a good blend: magnificent and maddening, generous and demanding, magnanimous and touchy, conceited and shy, resentful and demure; they were, at the same time, crass materialists and confirmed believers in the spirit world. Their gift for maintaining good human relationships was uncanny, surpassing anything I had met in Western industrial public relations or full-gospel community chapels. As for the buildings, they were completely wired for electricity, which we bought from the municipality 6:30 to 10:30 every evening. And the staff houses boasted flush toilets.

But not infrequently some aspect of my professional assignment itself caused considerable frustration, demanding of me to draw on every personal resource for a solution and on resources outside myself.

There were days, particularly during the first year at Livingstone College, when I thought that little of my training and none of my experience in previous classrooms were of merit. Surely one of the by-products of my TAP experience is self-confidence gained through improvisation, and a greater appreciation of my abilities and limitations.

I faced problems uniquely African in nature: students of different tribe and tongue in the same classroom; students older than myself; young men and women reluctantly training to be teachers because more prestigious and demanding vocations fell to their peers more clever in intellect -- and politics; students who had studied biology and chemistry but still feared the ubiquitous spirits -- particularly the evil ones; and students whose parents and relatives were often illiterate and superstitious. Occasionally I entertained myself by imagining a PTA meeting held at Livingstone, where we might discuss "The Need for a Good Home Library in the Education of Every Pupil" -- or some other equally esoteric subject.

Many Livingstone students still retained that passion for acquiring the goddess of education so peculiar to primary school pupils in bush village schools, innocently agog at the world of the schoolroom, barren though I had seen it to be.

Jima Talume, one of the third-year fellows, was one such student who retained his passion for education. So earnest was he to be awarded a diploma that he was sorely tempted to sacrifice his Christian faith on the altar of secular education. All this he spilled out to me months after the headmaster one day had dismissed him from school, along with two other chaps right in the middle of my class. These three, and seven other fellows and girls were packed off to their homes on the first bus to pass the school gate with the instructions not to return until they brought with them the school's modest fee.

These fees, which seemed small to us Western teachers, were often a burden for the poorer students who succeeded in being placed in secondary schools or teacher training colleges like Livingstone.

Like most fathers Jima's could not provide enough money for school fees, and the school had let him remain on into the second term, without completing his payments on the first term. Suddenly, the headmaster decided on a showdown, to see if at least a few more shillings couldn't be shook loose from some relative in the students' families.

"One evening my mother told me that I would not be going back to Livingstone," Jima confided. "When I asked her why, she said that the family no longer had money for clothing and books and fees. She wanted me to become a doctor, but since I failed to get a pass on the Cambridge in biology and chemistry, she said I should study agricultural science. But I do not want to be an adviser to farmers."

"So you decided to try teaching," I queried.

"Yes," he replied languorously, a faraway look in his young eyes. "My great ambition was to study medicine for as long as it takes, perhaps with advance studies in London or Moscow. If that could have been the case, I would have tried my best to help or even improve health situations in my poor country, by influencing the government to establish more and more health centers, and by encouraging young people, even girls to study medicine. And to arouse their great interest in medicine, I would send out campaigns from health centers to instruct the villagers. I'd give demonstrations and show films on the subject. In that way I am sure the young people would have had a great desire to know how to get rid of common disease and they in turn would advise their own people on how to prevent disease."

As I listened to Jima, his voice rising with an old vision still much alive in his head, I could hear that he had not yet made his peace with his fate, and could see him in later years when he taught school he would still be thinking of himself as a brilliant medical student, inexplicably passed over.

On a biographic sketch he submitted for a composition assignment, Jima ended with words that echoed the same ambition: "I want to study medicine. That is my burning desire. And I shall do it, for I am optimistic. True, as an alternative, I am studying to be a teacher now. But that too some day shall be used -- when I teach medicine. I know my future at present seems vague, however I have every hope to some day go abroad to complete my studies in medicine. There is always sunshine behind a cloudy day. Amen."

"How did you get your fees?" My question plummeted him to the earth.

In reply, Jima told how he was sent to ask for assistance from his Uncle Ali Abu, an evangelical Muslim of some significance in his mother's village.

"Uncle Abu was willing to help — provided I become a Muslim," Jima said with a laugh. "Yes, now I can laugh about it, now that my family again has fallen on good times. But at that time it was a hard decision for me, a baptized Christian, poor, wanting desperately to get a degree, and not knowing which way to turn."

"So what did you do?"

"I returned home and dug in my mother's shamba for a week, when Uncle Abu himself came calling. I did not speak with him about the matter for another three days, but he found me one morning by the river and pressed me for a decision. I remember how I sat quietly for a while before saying, 'I want to be a Christian.' And from that moment on, he has treated me coldly, though not bitterly."

"But tell me, Jima, were you really temped by your Uncle Abu's offer?" I asked, a bit stupidly perhaps, unable to let the discussion go.

"It was like . . . my Gethsemane," he said, looking away.

I might have known, for the lust for education is strong in the blood of African youth; it is **les rites de passage** from the doldrums of an isolated village to firm footing within the twentieth century urban Africa. How strongly Jima saw education setting himself off from his more unfortunate peers was reflected in another personal essay, which was badly written. It started out to be a tribute to a Christian education at Livingstone, its purposes, its facilities, its staff, but ended on a strange tribute to me.

"My schooling at Livingstone has changed my life very much for I seem to be a bit more civilized than other boys who failed to go on with schooling due to financial or intellectual problems. My family believes in the Presbyterian Church. My father plays a big part in this church for he is a church elder. Religion has changed our life very much, for my grandfather and grandmother were drunkards, fond of fighting and doing all sorts of evils and superstitions. It is beginning with my father that our progresses generate, for he is not only an elder but a teacher. Without education and religion, we would still be following what my grandfather and grandmother were doing.

"During my stay here at Livingstone Teachers College, I have come to know and admire many fine Christian teachers, particularly Mr. Hiebert. Through him, I understand the American way of life and also learned to like English literature for its own sake. He is a tall, easy-going, happy-go-lucky, and good-looking chap in his mid-twenties, with an intelligent and experienced mind.

"At first, I was fascinated by his gay, easy-going, ever-smiling manners and his sense of humor. He appeared happy in every circumstance and always cracked some jokes. Though sometimes we students could not understand what he laughed at so uproariously. But we laughed too. Yet, he is a very industrious man. He raised the photography club from nothing to the most popular and educative society in the school by his own hand, and revived the singing choir to hitherto unsurpassed heights by leading the voices to win the coveted regional prize in a singing contest.

"In the same way he raised Kaunda House from a dirty, old, usually uncooperative house to be a clean, beautiful, and admired dormitory. He helped in sports and community service, and he is a very good basketball player, a game which he introduced with enthusiasm to Livingstone students.

"Although I hate English poetry, I believe he taught it well. I remember how he preached and quoted poetry everywhere.

"He has greatly contributed to both the student Christian movement and the Christian life of the school. A strong and active Christian himself, he encouraged and helped many students to understand more fully this matter of a Christian way of life.

"Finally, Mr. Hiebert was genuinely interested in Africans and the African way of life. He talked to me and my friends often on African politics and Africa's future. He visited several African homes and villages and helped students both academically and personally. Above all, he was a man with very strong principles and character."

Had Jima not been a moralist, with all the strength and weaknesses inherent to that position, I would have accused him of engaging in a bit of old-fashioned apple-polishing. But he was such an impeccable moralist that I knew no impure motive behind the writing of the essay sullied his character.

Jima was only one of many African students who learned that acquiring a liberating education was not a magic solution to all problems. Catherine Shinyanga was another. Because of some trouble with a man in her village, there were extended doubts about permitting her to return to Livingstone after her first year. But she convinced the headmaster that she had reformed and had received great cleansing by the Blood. So back she came, for the church and its missionaries liked nothing better than penitent sinners.

Catherine's home is a mud-and-wattle, grass-roofed village on the slopes of Mitumba Mountain, 200 miles from the coast. To come to Livingstone she first walked fifteen miles down the mountain and through wooded savannah land to the nearest village served by a weekly bus. From there she rode thirty miles to a small town with a railway station. The last distance was covered by an overnight ride on the train and a four-mile bus ride or hike to the college.

The green slopes of that mountain were the setting for her early childhood, during which she learned the traditional customs and taboos of her tribe. But at the age of nine she was sent to a mission primary school seventy some miles from home. There she boarded for nine months each year. And that was the beginning of a distinction that set her off from most of the other girl members of her tribe. Primary led to middle school, a boarding school more than 100 miles from her village on the mountain.

Besides studying sciences and geography and history, she learned to speak the English language fluently, this in addition to knowing her tribal language and Swahili. Now she was at Livingstone in further studies.

She was a child of two worlds. And that might be a cliche, but to Catherine it was too often a humorless life. There was no easy resolutions between the cultural struggles of her two worlds; rather she had constantly to move between the world of traditional Africa and the world of a Western-oriented education for the technological age. At Livingstone she met students from a dozen different tribes and sat under teachers from a half-dozen different nations. Yet in her village to which she returned during school holidays, she lived with relatives who had never gone farther from the village than one day's walk.

"I don't want to go home this holiday," she once said to me. "Might you have work for me in the library during the holidays?"

"Do you need the money, that you wish to work during holidays?"

"No, it's that when I return to my village, I

have no one with whom to talk for five weeks."

Her compositions, which I had thought to be affected until that conversation about holiday work, showed the tension of inhabiting that marginal zone of two worlds. Hopefully, prayerfully, from that creative tension, students like Catherine will find the grace and honesty to embrace a new way of life that has blended the best of both worlds. It is an unenviable task, and one which I as her teacher could not show her how, having never dwelt there myself.

But dark-eyed, fawn-like Catherine became a casualty to the new freedom the educated, liberated young African woman inherits. With the old animistic mores gone, and the new liberty in Christ so frighteningly intangible, she missed a step on her way up and had to leave school during the second term of her last year to have her illegitimate child. She returned to take the examinations, which she will likely pass, but then I wondered where we at Livingstone College had failed her in helping her to pass that more crucial test.

Some on the staff thought her demure smile to be a guise of a beguiling wench. Others thought her to be charming, and the hapless victim of some fat lecher, whose name she was frightened to divulge. I suppose I thought of Catherine as being a mixture of pagan and Christian, a mixture she was not yet so adroit at hiding as the more hypocritical among us at Livingstone. Mostly I did not think of her morals, but rather of her love for English literature. She devoured Shakespeare, and her vocabulary excited faint jealousy among her classmates.

A British English text we used included the following Shakespeare sonnet:

That time of year thou may'st in me behold
When yellow leaves, or none, or few, do hang
Upon those boughs which shake against the cold,
Bare ruined choirs, were late the sweet birds sang.

In me thou see'st the twilight of such day
As after sunset fadeth in the west,
Which by and by black night doth take away,
Death's second self, that seals up all in rest.

In me thou see'st the glowing of such fire.
That on the ashes of his youth doth lie
As the deathbed whereon it must expire,
Consumed with that which it was nourished by.

-- This thou perceiv'st, which makes thy love more
       strong.
To love that well which thou must leave ere long.

While the meaning of the last lines was grasped after only the simplest explanation of King James' English, the metaphor referring to autumn and twilight stumped Catherine, as well as the class. Only after the use of pictures of flaming New England sugar maples clipped from old magazines, and the most explicit description of the chemical change of chlorophyll in leaves could the students understand the concept of seasonal change of colors and falling leaves. There was still the matter of twilight to be cleared up for students living on or so closely to the equator that for them when the flaming sunsets faded, black night came down immediately. There was no lingering twilight, as in Shakespeare's cold northern country, or as in mine.

The fabled African student displaying eagerness, seriousness, and an intense desire to achieve mostly by now has gone the way of the dodo. In his place is a student expecting every academic morsel to be served up by his teacher on a plate of excellence, and heavily sauced with gimmicks for easy retention.

Many of the students had poor study habits, relying mostly on learning by rote. Although I took the time repeatedly to show them how to study more effectively, few ever adopted the methods. Most stuck to the old practice of memorizing an endless stream of notes the teacher would write daily on the blackboard, and further expected him to dig out anything which mattered seriously by the syllabus or in light of the examinations. Too frequently these demanding attitudes of the students tended to offset the fine sense of satisfaction I had come to expect from earlier teaching situations, or else killed any Samaritan feelings altogether.

The students kept notebooks on every subject they studied, in which they copied their teachers' notes from the blackboards of a dozen rooms, and which in turn had to be regularly checked by the teachers. It was a pedagogical device so diabolically entrenched at Livingstone that any rookie daring to lecture, or worse yet, discuss, without first chalking the boards with academic hieroglyphics was subject to cacophonies of students in distress. It was enough to drive the TAP teacher to drink, throwing his MCC vows of abstinence to the winds.

When night after night at Livingstone, while my wife read novels and experimented with African recipes on a charcoal stove in her kitchen, I sat correcting notebooks, notebooks, and more notebooks, I would ask myself: has it been worth leaving the States for three years to teach at an isolated mission post in Africa? Has it been worth getting up for seven-thirty o'clock classes, and to end that day -- and a hundred more to come -- by a nightly ritual of drudgery among columns and columns of student notebooks filled with innocuous essays and their garbled regurgitations of my notes of wisdom? And burn more midnight oil of kerosine in one year, after the lights went out at ten-thirty, than in four years of college and three years of courtship?

Was I frustrated? Yes and no! Mostly I reminded myself that these were the reasons for TAP existing: assisting a new nation to educate its people and to develop its educational resources. Were there no problems, TAP could go home. In the morning I usually had a new vision of my work and influence. But not always, for another brush with Tom Njembi could wipe out any glimmer of a vision.

Tom was cynical, touchy, and without any redeeming quality of humor. He was a bitter essence drawn from the darkest brews of African tribalism and despotism. During a time of national crisis when one tribe lost its national sense and suddenly reverted to expressions of stronger loyalties to themselves, it was Tom who infected Livingstone campus with the evil contagion of tribalism.

One afternoon during a crucial football match with the boys from a nearby secondary school, a Livingstone player suffered an injury and was forced to leave the field early. While limping to his dormitory, he had his life threatened by a group of fellows, led by Tom.

"You're a traitor!" they hissed. "A traitor to your country and the school. Your kind must be killed, now, before your tribe can arm itself to fight the nation."

The injured player protested his innocence amid jeers and curses.

"And you're a traitor to Livingstone, too! You're not hurt! You only wanted our school to lose the game to those other fellows!"

Many of the members of the team playing against our Livingstone fellows in that particular match were indeed from the offending tribe. Tom had mistakenly concluded that since the Livingstone footballer bore no facial marks, as common to the people of Livingstone vicinity, he must therefore be from the tribe in rebellion. The footballer was actually from a tribe of no national or regional consequence, some distance from our area. Fortunately, some students happened along at the time of Tom's threatening assault and saved the injured footballer from a beating.

While Tom got sent home to his village for the remainder of that term, it was the other chap who suffered the most in the end. When the new term resumed he did not show up. Only after the headmaster himself sought out the fellow did we learn that he had entered another college in another region among members of another tribe.

However, most of the students at Livingstone genuinely made gallant attempts to subdue their tribal loyalties, and the staff sought to introduce Christ as the supreme unifying factor among the sons of men. But I honestly admit that many times I doubted that the fellows and girls at Livingstone experienced such an ideal. Too often their tribal loyalties seemed distended to their extremities to understand how comprehensive nationalism was in its demands, let alone how nonnational or international were the claims of Christ.

In the classroom, Tom yawned or scowled during discussions, and resented every assignment, often smartly suggesting how they should be revised. Since the students were teachers-in-training, they were conscious of teaching methods, and critical of classroom procedures, but none so cheeky in his criticism as Tom. Once during an unusually rash gush from Tom on how to modify a certain project being assigned, I interrupted him by saying, "Stop speaking such rubbish!"

He sprang from his seat, trembling with shock. "Rubbish! Rubbish, sir? Did you call me rubbish?"

"Sit down, Tom," I said calmy but firmly. "I did not call **you** rubbish. I described the stupid remarks you said as being rubbish."

"And what is the difference, sir?" He exploded again, this time from his seat. "My words are me!"

And suddenly a memory started jangling up, a memory of having read something which said that Africans frequently have trouble accepting criticism of their writings, their speeches, or their ideas. To criticize any of those is to criticize them personally. For the words, written or spoken, and the ideas, are only an extension of themselves. They seemed to have little of the Western concept that to judge a man's idea or product is not to judge his character.

All the students were syllabi-conscious, and wary of any prolonged discussion which grew out of the lesson but which in the strictest academic sense was only incidentally related. In many ways the African classroom was for me a reverse of my American classroom. By that I mean, in the States the students often attempted to shift the class discussion off the poem or short story under consideration and on to other topics such as politics, fads, latest rock music, drugs, and the whole bit about a generation gap. In Africa, it was I as a teacher who tried to pry the students from the narrow rut of the syllabi to let their minds follow instinctive curiosity and ask why, to get them stimulated intellectually enough to pursue the larger philosophical and universal concepts behind the sheer mechanics of a poem or the permissive syntax employed, or the shades of meanings in the vocabulary.

"But it's not on the syllabus," they would rejoin under my prodding, worry on their faces.

"Will we be asked this on the examination?" they asked, a shadow of fear in their eyes.

"Perhaps not. But I'm trying to get you to think, to relate the various facts you learn to gain a new perspective, to organize the material in an orderly fashion, to produce a convincing argument. I'm not interested in pouring into your minds a jumble of facts for you to spin off later."

They rightly feared the stiff examinations at the end of their training, and while many failed, rarely could they accept it· personally. In Africa, the teacher is blamed for the student's failure.

Once I tried reasoning with Tom on the logic of such an accusation. He generally led the verbal assaults against the teachers whose students failed examinations.

"Perhaps a student failed because he had a poor grasp on the subject material," I began cautiously, attributing failure to lack of background instead of native intelligence. "Too often I as a teacher have the feeling that I am asked to erect an educational roof where there is no foundation poured. Then, too, each student has his own mental limitations."

"Sir, I can learn anything you can teach me!" And with that declaration by Tom of his intellectual prowess, I abandoned my attempt to discuss the matter rationally. And the students never forsook their belief that the teacher is at fault if his students fail.

I itched for the day they became teachers.

4. CLUBS:

Night and Day

The contact with students at Livingstone was too frequently limited to the formal rituals of the classroom, unless one worked quietly and persistently to modify the situation, because the educational system expected that teachers remain aloof. This troubled most American teachers -- including Evelyn and me -- who apparently feel the need to be loved and accepted by their students and colleagues, and repeatedly recognized for their good deeds. The English and the continental European teachers seemed to thrive without such reassurances.

But there were plenty of opportunities to develop a relationship with the students outside the classroom, for those who felt the need, as well as for those who didn't. There were days and weeks on end when activities outside the classroom demanded as much of one's time as did the classroom. Since Livingstone, like most of the teacher training colleges and secondary schools in Africa, was a boarding school, there was, in addition to the student's education, the whole areas of his food, housing, and recreation with which to be concerned. To a North American teacher whose experience consisted of a clean seven-hour workday at the end of which he could neatly dispose of the students, and turn his back on his job for the rest of the day, TAP Africa with its boarding schools, and near 24-

hour duty, comes as a terrific jolt, even though the system was thoroughly discussed during orientation in America.

Evelyn and I were no exceptions. When at the beginning of the second month at the college I got socked with something called "Duty Teacher Week," a diabolical system not peculiar to Livingstone, I thought my professional career had fallen off the wagon somewhere and lay irreparably shattered in the dust.

In my role as Duty Teacher, I became the focus of student and staff hostilities alike. On the one hand, I was expected to defend the authority and dignity of the headmaster and honor the school as one of the last bastions of academic excellence with Christian principles. At the same time, I was expected to suppress the contumaciousness of the students, minister the mercy of God's grace in chapels and the judgment of the school's law during evening prep, and preserve the Livingstone virgins from forays by our own fellows. There were cooks to prod, gardeners to mollify, patrons to entertain, and otherwise -- if there was time or energy -- Lucifer to repulse!

Much that passes in North America as extracurricular activities or social functions of the school is an intense learning experience for the student in Africa. There were opportunities to introduce them to new games, such as basketball or volleyball, or perhaps give them their first taste of photography, astronomy, piano, or oil painting. The TAP teacher, who may have had little interest, ability, or experience in any one of those fields, soon found himself deeply involved in them, and enjoying them greatly, thanks to the slot in the schedule for clubs on Friday afternoons.

Livingstone's spread of clubs, at least one of which was compulsory for each student -- though some managed to swing three or four -- included a drama guild, a monthly newssheet and the yearly magazine (as they called their equivalent of the yearbook), the Student Christian Organization, a band, Girl Guides and Boy Scouts, a mixed choir, a photography club, an astronomy organization, Young Farmers Club, a library committee, a hikers association, an art club, and a French language club. All of which needed to have teachers as sponsors.

The choir, the photography club, the library committee, and the ill-fated hikers organization fell to my lot. Evelyn got stuck with art and Girl Guides.

But clubs were not the sole out-of-class activities in which student and teacher got equally enmeshed. Additionally, for the teachers, were job assignments such as sportsmasters, classmasters, dormitory-masters, dining hall supervisor, the school store, the library, the electrical system and pumping plant, medical director, school vehicle logistics, the school's bookkeeping, supervising the school's budding farm, preaching on the Sabbaths, overseeing small construction jobs, and assisting the headmaster with clerical work.

It remained a mystery to me for the full three

years I was at Livingstone, and still does to this day, why the college didn't hire one African man to carry many of these nonacademic assignments and free the teachers to pursue affairs worthy of their calling. Nevertheless, some of the best memories of teaching at Livingstone are from the after-hours talks with students as we worked in the library or in the improvised photographic dark-room, or on the attempted hikes.

As Jima recounted in his essay, I "revived the singing choir to hitherto unsurpassed heights by leading the voices to win the coveted regional prize in a singing contest." While the choir did bask in that acclaim, their invitation to travel to the capital to sing on the radio and television station was undoubtedly the pinnacle of their activity that year. It excited jealousy in other clubs, and a waiting list for vocal tryouts to join the choir amassed overnight.

The mixed-voice choir sacrificed their one short midterm holiday, remaining at Livingstone so they could rehearse every day. A week before the new school term I took them to the capital for the program. Not only was it their first time to ap-pear on television, but also for the most of them, it was their first trip to the capital. The irony, of course, is that almost none of their families or relatives owned TV sets and thus missed the debut of their kin.

Not all the requests to have the school choir perform publicly were rewarding experiences. In preparation for a three-day celebration on the oc-

casion of the official opening of the Bishop Cart-
wright Memorial Theological College, in a neighboring town, I began special training of the choir only
to come down with hepatitis. Following a month's
convalescence, I dragged back into the classroom
with only two weeks before the big event, knowing
that I could not possibly have them in shape by
then. This was early in the school year before we
had many rehearsals, and before the midterm holiday practices preparing for the TV program.

Though I had sung in college choirs and had
taken piano lessons for years right into my late
teens, I was not a music major. Nevertheless, at
Livingstone, I was expected to make a great
contribution to the prestige of the school by
accomplishing many things in music: develop the
school choir; teach the entire student body to read
music from the scores so they could in turn teach
it properly to primary or middle school students;
instruct thirty organ students so they could be used
in their church; correct the many mistakes in the
English hymns and translations they already knew;
teach them new hymns; and train them in singing
the Anglican liturgical chants.

I would have enjoyed working at many of those
great expectations, but I was given one forty-minute
period every Tuesday afternoon to teach music
to the whole student body of more than 200.

"I am sorry, Mr. Hiebert, but it is the only
provision in the timetable for music teaching,"
the headmaster said without much conviction.

When we arrived at Livingstone we found that the other male TAP teacher had been assigned the leadership of the Young Farmers Club, whose thirty-five members were all fellows, though traditionally much of the menial shamba work at the village level was still carried by the women. The club raised chickens and planted a vegetable garden. In the previous term each member had a vegetable plot; and for the past two terms they raised three sets of thirty-five chickens. The vegetables were sold to the school for use in the kitchen; the chickens were sold to staff members, local African people, and a few in town. The last year we were there, the Young Farmers Club was experimenting with raising 100 broilers and with introducing a new method of growing vegetables.

One of the changes the first African headmaster established was the expansion of the Young Farmers Club's vegetable plots into a large school garden, with every student having to spend some time each week working in it under the supervision of the club. The aim was for Livingstone College to become self-sufficient in the production of vegetables and bananas, hopefully with enough left over to sell for a profit.

The school sought the assistance of the regional agricultural agent, who surveyed the land and recommended what should be planted. The job of clearing the land of thorn scrub and tall, coarse-bladed grass to plant five acres of bananas and five of vegetables seemed almost too much for the students. But every day a group of students with a teacher or two worked in the garden, and slowly through the weeks one could see the bush being rolled back.

Teachers were not to be merely overseers, standing with hands on hips and surveying the scene of students digging and raking, like some plantation Bwana supervising his peasants. We joined the students, the school being divided into several groups, each group with two teachers who were members of that group.

One day we dug in the garden, another day we went to village corrals to buy manure, and on another day it was burning the dry thorn branches. To see their white teachers and their own educated people digging with broad hoe or slinging manure was a shocking surprise for many of the students. Too many had assumed that educated persons don't dirty their hands. The involvement on the part of us teachers was most necessary to aid in the change of attitudes toward manual labor.

During my second year at Livingstone, I attempted to form a hikers club which included general nature hikes, bird hikes, and mountain hikes. A few yards beyond the north side of the school boundary one entered a near primeval bush country, and while there were none of those exotic animals peculiar to Africa anywhere near at hand, nor even antelope, one could find brilliant lizards and rock connies and birds of all colors flashing sunlight off their wings. Any nature lover, I assumed, would revel in a quiet afternoon's tracking of such wildlife.

The brooding, purple hills to the east begged for

exploration, as did the inselberg, those strange bald outcropping of brown-stained granite boulders lying on the plains, warm under the sun. The joints between had weathered away more rapidly than the granite core of the blocks, producing fantastic shapes.

A few fellows joined blindly, having never heard of such a club. Outward Bound, they had heard of, where boys pitted their strength against the elements of nature to harden themselves and train themselves for survival. The Boy Scouts were familiar to them where one might also do some feats of strength against nature. But a club for hiking just for the sake of enjoying the hike and the environs through which one hiked? It was unheard of.

Thus, it was of no surprise to the old-timers at Livingstone, that my first hike with a handful of fellows was a total disaster.

One afternoon we struck out through the bush to the nearest inselberg, a brown stubby finger rising from the plains four miles away. But as we approached the hilly rock cluster and began to ascend, the boys found it difficult to understand why we should be climbing it when it would be much easier to go around the inselberg.

"If my parents were to hear about this hike, I would be ridiculed," one fellow volunteered, embarrassment edging his voice.

The view from the plateau of the hill was stunning, but little of its grandeur seeped into my disillusioned group of reluctant hikers sprawled at my feet. For the route home I had planned a visit to a small gorge slightly off the direct line between the inselberg and the school. After we had been walking for another hour, one of the fellows straggled up beside me and asked:

"Please, sir, where are we going?"

"Well," I said brightly, stopping briefly to boost morale, "we're not really going anywhere. We're hiking across here a mile or so to explore this gorge I've been talking about."

He looked at me with a baffled expression, scratched his perspiring head, and turned away. The best I could gather was that he seemed to think that we should have some purpose or destination in mind for our walking, that one could not just hike about for pleasure. I learned that afternoon the the different values America and Africa placed on certain functions and objects. Walking, like women's breast in Africa, served a purpose; neither existed for pleasure. In overdeveloped America, where technology has given man wheels to cover all distances, walking became a sport; and Western culture assigned a sexual appeal to the mammary gland after woman found an "advanced" method of feeding her offspring.

Another enjoyable but time-consuming out-of-classroom activity of mine for a year was tutoring a Portuguese-speaking black from Mozambique who was falling further and further behind in his English classes. I tried to match his earnestness by finding time each day to privately tutor Peter until he could comprehend more of what was going on in class.

Peter claimed to be a member of the Revolutionary Government of Mozambique in Exile, and that prior to fleeing his country he had for two years taken part in actual guerrilla skirmishes. All during his high school years, he was given the job of monitoring the radio for the revolutionaries, relaying and receiving messages for them. At the end of his third year, he and his brother were allowed to join the guerrillas in the hinterlands.

During practices in English conversation, he told of helping to blow up bridges, ambushing the Portuguese, mining roads at night, burning government outposts, and ransacking an occasional plantation.

"The guerrilla way of life was hard," he volunteered. "But we found our comfort in religion."

"You mean in Christianity?" I asked, surprised, for I thought he was a practicing Catholic. "The same religion of the white man you were fighting?"

"Yes, we do not associate Christianity with the Portuguese colonialists. There are many Christian guerrillas, and before going into a battle, we all pray together, Catholic and Protestant alike, in the free way of you Protestants."

"What do you answer the people who advise revolutionaries to work at peaceful methods for throwing off colonialism?"

"It is a foolish conception. We cannot afford that luxury. We have submitted for four centuries to these Portuguese people, and how has our country

71

progressed? Portugal itself is a backward country among European nations. She cannot possibly help us. We know that, for we read, and hear, and see how other European countries had ruled their African territories better."

On another occasion, Peter told that the hardest part about living under a colonial government was being treated always as a child. Paternalistic, he might have called the Portuguese colonialists, had he known that English word.

Peter turned up at Livingstone with a fair smattering of English, asking to continue his studies, and only gradually over the months did we piece his story together. He had been with a band of guerrillas near the border of Mozambique and our country when he was shot in the leg. Friends helped him over the border to safety and to a mission hospital where he had the bullet removed and remained for convalescence. He had decided to perfect his English, and finish his education, all the while. keeping in touch with the guerrilla activity through his membership in the Revolutionary Government of Mozambique in Exile. I suspected that he was being groomed by the revolutionaries to be another propagandist for Mozambique freedom causes to the English-speaking world.

While TAP teachers in other countries, particularly Nigeria, made frequent trips into the bush on preaching or Sunday school teaching missions, little or none of that kind of extracurricular activity was ours at Livingstone. A student work camp I helped organize was the nearest experience to what my colleagues in West Africa enjoyed.

Wallace didn't know what to think of the idea when I invited him and a few other fellow students to a work camp during part of their midterm holiday.

"A work camp? Me? I'm a student!"

I spared him the agony of explaining what that meant, for I knew many thought that students were not to be caught with a shovel or a hoe, except for a bit of forced self-help the college was able to pull off. I only smiled at him and waited for what I was sure would be the better spirit eventually coming through in him.

"Oh, well, maybe I'll try it."

"Good, get about six or eight of your friends."

Later, Wallace hopped onto the back of the school truck with five other Livingstone students, several boys from the theological college nearby, three teachers, a pastor, the other TAP teacher, and an English missionary. We struck out for an interior village north of Mbala where an African pastor's house and church were completely destroyed in a flood during the last rainy season. All that remained were the foundations and a few crumbling walls.

On arrival Wallace and the other students helped us all unpack in some huts the pastor had hastily erected following the flood. We counselors cooked on a kerosine burner, obtained water from a barrel replenished by some village women, and slept on mats on the dirt floors.

The Livingstone fellows soon entered into the relaxed, communal spirit of a work camp. By their attentiveness, they showed appreciation for the early morning devotions with the village people conducted in the local dialect, in which God's Word was refreshingly clear to them.

After a slim breakfast, everyone put on his old shorts, picked up hand tools, and hovered about the English missionary for instructions. Then it was a long morning of carrying stones for the walls, mixing mud for the masons, cutting rafters and re-landscaping the washed-out areas about the small church and home.

At noon everyone joined in for a good heavy African meal of thick mush, seasoned beef stew, and banana cakes with tea. Then the local pastor conducted a Bible study, centering his lessons on salvation and the events surrounding the death of the Lord. One afternoon the fellows experimented with "buzz" groups, a novel learning situation for them, in which they were to share insights on the Beatitudes.

Later in the afternoons, students and counselors joined in a wild soccer melee, and on one occasion hiked two miles for a swim. When the students arrived at the river they stripped and jumped in for their first thorough bath in five days. The other TAP teacher and I followed them cautiously, remembering all the stories about crocodile-infested rivers of the tropics and disease-carrying snails.

Wallace liked the campfire each night the best, for it revived for him and the other students the village days of their youth, before they got sent off to middle schools and teacher training colleges. Every night there was singing, with my fellow TAP colleague playing some American folk songs on his guitar or the Africans singing their own to the accompaniment of a few small hand drums. Other nights were spent in swapping folklore and riddles, doing pantomimes, or discussing African politics. The last campfire service ended on a serious tone, with questions and testimonies.

The next morning, when the truck started back to Livingstone, the village people lined the pathway waving and laughing. They would miss this strange bunch of students and teachers who had descended on their village for a week, but mostly, I hoped, they would remember our presence as an encouragement to their Christian faith.

Both in the classroom and out of the classroom there was much, much work for the TAP teacher, and his American sense of industry and urgency tempted him sorely to slug out long hours to accomplish more. But in Africa, many of the TAP-ers, as did Evelyn and I, learned how much more important being is than doing, and relationship is than accomplishment. In the school clubs one found less pressure to perform, to produce, to accomplish, and thus, with a relaxed pace on occasion to relate, to trust, to enjoy. One became less interested in whether the year after he left the school was still using a revised English syllabus he had prepared.

He learned that what mattered more was whether the Livingstone College students had seen a difference in his life, and knew that it was the Christ who dwelled within.

TAP
PHOTO
ALBUM

The pictures on the following
pages are of teachers and students
in various activities in the
Teachers Abroad Program (TAP)
in Africa.

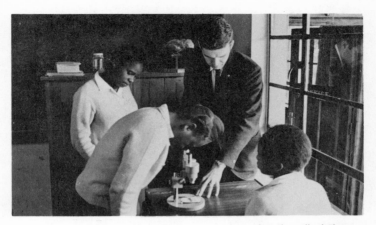

Photo by Willard Claassen

Murray Snider in the classroom at the Girls' High School, Kijabe, Kenya

Photo by Willard Claassen

John Shenk (center) and the headmaster (left) at Githumu Secondary School, Thika, Kenya

Photo by Willard Claassen
Kahuhia Girls' High School, Fort Hall, Kenya

Photo by Willard Claassen
Alliance Secondary School, Dodoma, Tanzania

80

Photo by Willard Claassen

Loretta (left) and Murray (standing) Snider relax with other teachers at tea at Girls' High School, Kijabe, Kenya

Photo by Willard Claassen

Janet Kortemeier and Hershey Leaman at the Mosoriot Teacher Training College at Eldoret, Kenya

Photo by Willard Claassen
Grace Gehman, Tanga Secondary School, Tanzania, 1970

Photo by Willard Claassen

John Hofstetter, Livingstonia, Malawi, 1971

Photo by Willard Claassen

Henry Jackson coaches athletics at the Kijabe High
School, Kenya

Photo by Willard Claassen

Henry Jackson's students going through their exercises
at Kijabe High School, Kenya

Photo by Willard Claassen

Milton Troyer and his self-reliance program of raising chickens, Dodoma, Tanzania

Photo by Willard Claassen

Milton Troyer giving guidance in the self-reliance program in chicken raising, Dodoma, Tanzania

Photo by Willard Claassen

Colin Mishler, Ambiva Secondary School, Kisumu, Kenya, 1971

Photo by Willard Claassen

Lois Shenk making a fire for hot water in their house
at Githumu Secondary School, Thika, Kenya

87

Photo by Willard Claassen

Jean Snyder and Miriam Stoltzfus with the headmistress at the Tumutumu Girls' High School, Karatina, Kenya

Photo by Willard Claassen

John Shenk and student in front of boys' dormitory at Githumu Secondary School, Kenya

Photo by Willard Claassen

Ron Mathias, Henry Henderson Institute, Blantyre, Malawi, 1971

Photo by Willard Claassen

Leroy Williams, Livingstonia, Malawi, 1971

Photo by Willard Claassen

Janet Kortemeier at the Mosoriot Teacher Training College at Eldoret, Kenya

Photo by Willard Claassen

Ron Mathies, Henry Henderson Institute, Blantyre, Malawi, 1971

Photo by Willard Claassen

Cleaning dormitories at Githumu Secondary School, Thika, Kenya

5. RENEWAL:

Prayers and Teas

My introduction to religious activities in Africa was colorful and romantic; something right out of the old missionary books. I would have been better off without that novel preface to my TAP experience.

Evelyn and I had arrived at Livingstone Teachers College nearly a week before the opening term. The days were spent with shopping for kerosine, mosquito nets, and papaya, and looking over strange textbooks and syllabi. Though not a teacher in the college, a young missionary, a kind of anthropologist-evangelist, lived on the campus. That first weekend he made a motorcycle trip deep into the bush and had invited me to ride along with him. His wife took Evelyn under her wing for a seminar on housekeeping in Africa.

I hugged the rear half of a motorcycle seat as we bashed along on the dirt road, swerving madly to avoid potholes and goats, and spraying the little chips of gravel under the fat tires. I was agog as bush-village-savannah Africa streamed past like a surrealistic painting alive on the canvas. And at the end of the ride with night already coming down there was a genuine camp-out to boot.

We sat on our haunches in front of one of those typical round grass-roofed, mud huts which peppers the letters and slide-lectures of a thousand missionaries to Africa, and which peppers the landscape of the African savannah. The only light was the glowing embers of a wood fire over which the evening stew simmered. While the men tied up the milk cows for the night, the herdboys secured their flocks in thorn-fenced corrals.

The night's freshness had not yet crept up from the soil to wipe out the village dust caught in the throat, nor the heavy odor of cow dung in the nostrils. Yet there under a bowlful of warm stars spilled overhead, the anthropologist-evangelist spoke to the families about God. As I listened, with an occasional hurried translation whispered to me, I learned something of the life of the people, and their great spiritual needs beyond the most obvious physical needs I could see.

"There are literally dozens of villages throughout this district without one national Christian living in them," the missionary said to me later. "And neither a national pastor nor a missionary visits them, their time being consumed with running the institutions they've erected."

Is there any wonder that visions of pioneer missionary work danced in my head as I lay in the darkness trying to sleep? I saw myself peddling along the sandy paths from village to village, my bicycle tires bald with my efforts to get out the gospel. The ease with which the anthropologist-evangelist blended God-talk with village discussions that night triggered in me a spiritual longing to become that kind of witness, a longing which did not die with the first wash of dawn.

The return to Livingstone and the mounting of

its obligations tempered the vision. In another month, strangely enough, it was religion itself which buried the longing forever.

A mission school such as Livingstone too easily becomes a religious ghetto, a snug European-oriented community who looks upon itself as a kind of spiritual buoy joggling on the crest of a pagan black wave. The twice-daily obligatory chapels, the opening prayers for every occasion, the staff prayer meetings, the compulsory Bible Knowledge classes, plus all the regularly scheduled sabbath activities were too many for the good of the students, and even for the good of the white missionaries. It violated that necessary balance between corporate and private acts of worship. Even the nonacademic activities of the school, set in this artificial religious environment, seemed too frequently geared to supporting the white mission establishment.

One was told endlessly by the senior missionary teachers what a privilege it was to live on such a large station with his fellow colleagues, instead of being stuck away in a village alone. But Evelyn and I found increasingly the faith of many of our colleagues to be dull though febrile, and joined a young British couple in arranging a biweekly encounter session in which African, English, and American teachers and community folk could gather to discuss religious and personal problems. Were it not for the anthropologist-evangelist and his wife, and Sospeter, a fellow African colleague, with whom Evelyn and I felt free to be frank, we would have found it hard to avoid cynicism, perhaps even to keep our faith -- in the church and her bungling attempts at being obedient to a divine mandate of world mission. Most of the other staff members were either not of a speculative or reflective sort, or else needed the security of traditional worship and witness patterns too greatly to risk participating in the candor of personal criticism. Many of the presumed spiritual battles fought at Livingstone were little more than skirmishes on minor issues with fellow Christians instead of major onslaughts against the non-Christian forces.

"Funny, how conversations with Catholics and non-Christians are often more refreshing," a fellow TAP-er said at a retreat four months after Evelyn and I had arrived in Africa. And how we wanted to chorus a hearty Amen!

In this stagnant, fairly negative religious atmosphere of Livingstone sprang two good side effects. One's personal devotions took on new life. During the times of private reflection and meditation one found that the urgent shaft his spirit thrust down was rewarded with fountains of living waters. He learned, perhaps for the first time, what the psalmist meant when he wrote: "All my springs are in thee."

A lesson in tolerance was the other good aspect. Because of the varying backgrounds of the Christian teachers, one needed to become a more expansive soul, possessing a greater tolerance and better understanding for the different behavior and practices. Greater emphasis now could be placed on being Christian, as against being only Mennonite.

Here Evelyn and I found ourselves moving away from provincial denominationalism and toward international Christian brotherhood; yet oddly enough, while working in the Livingstone setting, we became more strongly convinced about our Mennonite faith. It was not a situation we expected to dissolve easily, but hoped that from such tension our faith might spring up freshly again and again.

The African student generally seems not to have made up his mind about the Christian faith. Some few would regard it as superficial and are not impressed by religious trappings and pomp. While most would call themselves Christian, like their Western counterparts, their faith is often a veneer, rarely touching the psychic reflexes and impulses. Since many of the schools are still church-operated, the student is in a situation where Christianity may seem to be taken for granted. Once the state takes over the public education of its youth, and if specific Christian teaching gets ruled from the curriculum, then will come the test for the truly Christian student, and teacher alike.

Without a doubt, the religious highlight of my TAP experience was a Christian Leadership Course I participated in. I learned to know the Christian youth of the country in a way impossible at Livingstone. Held during school holidays, attendance was voluntary. That fact alone set the proper mood, since so much of the African student's religious activities were obligatory.

I was one of twelve leaders -- six African and six expatriate -- who helped head prayer and

Bible study groups daily and lead discussions on the theme of the course: "He Makes All Things New." The 125 students, representing seven tribes, were divided into twelve groups. The coordinator of the course assigned each of us twelve leaders to a group. For six days -- the length of the leadership course -- we leaders lived with our individual groups, eating African food together, discussing marriage, vocation, church, and nation together, sleeping in student dormitories, and joining in volleyball and hikes.

The whole course was designed to help train these students to lead such activities on their own once they returned to their own schools and villages. Many of them were struggling for clarity of truth about their Christian faith. They expressed concerns of how to witness to their pagan or Muslim families, and how to relate the Christian faith to nationalism. Discussions were lively and intensely personal.

A week with such African Christian students as these at the leadership course did much to offset the spiritual miasma at Livingstone. With such students, too, it was possible to accent personal relations, and bridge that awesome gap between a teacher and his pupils, as perpetrated by the British in particular. Relationships between expatriates and the Africans were fairly normal, at least one saw little open friction. But, also, rarely did one see warm friendships developing naturally between the two parties. And much of blame for that could rightfully be placed on the

European, if the European teaching staff at Livingstone was representative. From all that I heard and observed, I doubt that we were peculiar.

Evelyn and I came to Africa to teach in a teacher training college, to help the Christian church, to travel, and to learn about African people. However, to get to know the Africans, to have social contact with them was nigh impossible. We found that most of the white people did not associate with the Africans outside of a certain professional or formal relationship.

At Livingstone, the white community invited each other for teas and evening games, but the Africans were left out. Most of the European teachers, especially the British, expressed astonishment when we implied a desire to have more contact with the Africans.

"But after you've worked with them all day, it would be bloody fatiguing to have them in yet for tea," they'd say, throwing up a surprised hand. "Surely you can understand that. People quite naturally drift to their own kind for social functions."

There was a high incidence of boredom among the teachers, particularly the Americans. The younger ones, including another TAP couple, seemed childish in their restlessness; they were truly children of the technological West. Over-stimulated, dashing about to cram every leisure spot with high activities, or to be spectators of others in the same mad pursuits, they were lost in Africa with leisure time on their hands and having no intense avocational interest personally, or native curiosity about their novel environs. "The White Whirl" is how Evelyn and I dubbed the social life at our school. We are not the type of people who require great flurries of social engagements; we're quite happy to get alone with our books and diaries and sewing. Yet, other teachers seemed so bored with themselves that they must tea everybody every day.

We tried to change this social precedent by inviting Africans to our home for meals. Poor Sospeter, how often he was our social guinea pig in attempts to bridge the social gap. Two years passed before we had our first meal in an African home. Too frequently they assume that we European teachers would not accept an invitation or would not appreciate a visit to their home.

It was a strange dilemma. If one tried to avoid the white whirl cliques there was no guarantee he'd fare better with the Africans. Thus, one ended up the years with developing few close friendships either European or African.

There were Americans in the area not related to Livingstone College, and we found ourselves together occasionally. I remember particularly the Peace Corps teachers, young adults like myself, but who were searching for the "truth." Opportunities to share with them at such levels, while not frequent, were vigorous. Such encounters, without a doubt, contributed to the growth of my own faith. But I did not want to go almost halfway around the world to end up talking endlessly with typical American university kids.

Evelyn and I did get in one outside social function with Africans that first year. A half brother of Grace, our house servant, got married in the nearby town. We found ourselves attending the wedding of perfect strangers, and a bit put on display by Grace, as we were the only whites besides another older missionary couple. It was a strange mixture of people. Near clothesless in-laws down from the hills mingled with the town-wise bureaucrats and the royalty of the house of the chief.

For the occasion, the role of master and servant was switched as Grace took us under her wing and ushered us to a front pew past hundreds of other people unable to get into the tiny church. Our protests were to no avail; we could only hope that the spectators squeezed in doorways and windows saw how humbled and penitent we looked.

Our meager Swahili was insufficient for most of the long sermon. When the pastor placed his hand over those of the bride and groom, we got a good idea of what was going on. And the moment seemed as big to those two amid the dust and insects and faded religious pictures and cheap paper-chain decorations as it was for Evelyn and me in our opulent sanctuary with paneled mahogany and stained light and flaming candelabrum and fluting organ.

Fumbling for a pen to sign the marriage certificate, the pastor warned the newlyweds to make the marriage a good one because he wouldn't do the job again. It was an Anglican joke. As people coughed and scraped their sandals about restlessly on the gritty floor, he pulled off his crushed surplice and dark clerical robe, smiling and nodding to everyone and clasping his fat hands prayerfully before him. A guitar and accordion duet struck up "Jesus, Lover of My Soul" for a wedding march. And the party, self-contained and unsmiling, filed out of the church and marched down the church lane to a compound. The hundreds of well-wishers shuffling along stirred up a cloud of red dust.

The singing and chanting continued until the bridal party were seated under a canopy of banana leaves, a kind of miniature pavilion to ward off the smiting sun. Seated before a white tier-cake, baked for the occasion by the wife of the older missionary couple, the newly married folk received their gifts as people queued up to offer them. Plastic dishware, red and blue enameled basins, bananas, containers of cooking oil, a pillow, and some meters of cloth were among the gifts.

When night came down, we guests were served bowls of rice and beef stew with Pepsi Cola and a sweet biscuit. The drummers for dancing took over from the accordionist and guitarist for a full night's swinging, and Evelyn and I returned to Livingstone contentedly warmed by the event.

Our Western social ways were sometimes misunderstood by even those Africans whom we thought knew us the most intimately. The two-week visit of Peele's financee was one such example. Peele, a young English teacher with the Church Missionary Society and assigned to Livingstone, was engaged to an English missionary nurse stationed some hundreds of miles away. Mere weeks before their marriage, she came to Livingstone for a visit, staying with another English teacher couple.

Quite naturally, Peele spent all his free time with the girl -- hikes, picnics, and an occasional spin on a motorcycle. They were a lovely couple, sensitive to local customs, and foregoing what to Europeans would be permissible public expressions of romance.

But one morning, Grace, our house servant, confided to Evelyn that many of the African employees -- gardeners, cooks, school laundrymen -- were whispering about Peele and his fiancee.

"It's not good," Grace said, bewilderment in her face.

"What isn't?"

"Their being alone," she replied, shaking her head in sympathy with the gossipers.

"But they're nearly married, and both in their late twenties!"

"But they have been seen alone in Peele's house late at night."

"Well, of course. . . ."

"But you Europeans are very clever," Grace went on with a wise scowl. "I hear that you take pills to keep babies from coming."

Admitting that, Evelyn launched into a discussion about Western dating patterns, and Christian standards of courtship. Grace nodded her head and replied that she too was a Christian and knew what the church taught, but was also wise enough to know what went on when young men and women got alone like that.

"A Christian boy and girl in our village see each other openly," she said.

And though Evelyn pointed up the differences in social convention between African and American societies, and the expectations for Christian behavior within those systems, Grace remained unconvinced of Peele's innocence.

Not a month later she told Evelyn that her fifteen-year-old daughter was pregnant -- unmarried and unbetrothed.

"If only we Africans had some of those pills," she said bitterly.

Of course, the pill has invaded Africa, though perhaps little beyond the urban centers to the village level. And when that happens, African Christians will learn, as their European counterparts are learning, that the new freedom carries a heavy moral responsibility.

A teacher at Livingstone mixed socially with his students whenever an official school party was scheduled. There were parties whenever one of the sports teams won an important game or whenever some government official from the capital passed through or if some staff member was returning to his overseas home. After examinations, a big party was held for the senior class.

103

These school parties were African in flavor. The European administration sensibly kept its hand out of the planning. There were occasions for long speeches whose florid rhetoric was punctuated with thunderous shouts and stamps of acclaim from the audience. Great slabs of honeyed-bread were washed down with either too-sweet tea, Pepsi, or orange Fanta. Often a few old Victorian hymns got murdered by a student on an accordion, and an ensemble of fellows would demonstrate a tribal dance. But not every school party brought happiness. A fellow TAP teacher in the Congo once wrote to me:

"The exams went well for all our students except one. Characteristically, he blamed a professor for his failure and then accused three of us teachers of being hypocritical, for we had kept our promise to give a little party after they finished their examinations. However, this student figured that since he had failed we should have gone into mourning and refused to give a party.

"Activities for the evening included devotions, the meal, singing, movies, words of congratulations, and graduation presents.

"We were honored the following day by being invited by the students from another school to attend their banquet. But after that event, happiness that had been generated vanished.

"The graduating students felt that they were no longer subject to school rules, such as regulated hours for lights out, no smoking, and no drinking.

At the banquet, some of our students consumed alcoholic beverages. So, at the last minute, disciplinary measures were taken.

"On the day when the entire teaching staff should have been preparing a real feast and royal entertainment for the graduates, we were forced to have a meeting where the following decision was made: since you no longer consider yourselves to be our students, we must ask you to leave the school tomorrow morning. If you want to continue living in our dormitories, you must come and receive special permission to do so. Furthermore, the banquet to which you were invited has been canceled.

"The students were shocked. Unfortunately, their reaction got out of hand. So they left two days ahead of schedule."

While some of the religious and social incidents at Livingstone seem negatively or critically recounted here, they must be included to balance the TAP Africa picture, which tends to get romanticized on the North American side. When Evelyn and I came to the end of our three-year African sojourn, we trekked off to our American home honestly evaluating the TAP experience as a plus. We would gladly do it again, for we certainly had it better than our TAP friends at a secondary school. They were the only TAP teachers at their school, and also the sole Americans.

"We desperately want more TAP-ers here," they wrote. "Having someone to confide in who is both Christian and American could lighten some awfully heavy burdens. And this school needs qualified Christian teachers worse than the countryside needs rain!

"The British teachers are living up to the stereotype better than we first thought. The one makes himself unbearable with his perpetual stream of abusive, filthy chatter, which is usually directed against a white South African teacher. Of the seven African teachers, three seem genuinely dedicated to their profession, and the others generally to beer and women. Only one has stayed at this school for more than two years, and he is planning to leave.

"The school pretends to be Christian. Teachers preach to the students at assembly every school day, and of course on Sundays. Sunday evenings the students must go to bed early to keep from thinking evil on the Lord's Day. On Good Friday the students were expected to wear black or dark colors to mourn Christ's death, while some of their teachers gathered to drink beer just a few yards away. Yet, students will be expelled for drinking a beer, but teachers can carouse at nightlong booze parties. And more than one teacher has brought a town prostitute home Saturday night and then preached at the students in church the next morning.

"Bible ritual has replaced tribal ritual, and the idea of living one's Christianity somehow is slow at catching on."

6. TAP WIVES:

Classroom or Baby

And now the "I" turns feminine as I -- Evelyn -- stop looking over Jonathan's shoulder and strike the keyboard myself for this chapter on the TAP wife. My classroom experiences were similar to Jonathan's, so I shall write about other matters.

The school officially welcomed us with an outdoor tea held under the headmaster's mango trees. The white staff invited us to their homes for a round of meals and more teas and evenings of Scrabble, Rook, or slide viewings, and gave lots of advice on where to buy eggs and which day the town butchered and how to bargain and whether or not to employ a servant for our home. By the third week as the white whirl gained momentum I began to wonder where the African teachers' wives were.

"Please walk me down to Sospeter's home and introduce me to his wife," I begged a young Australian wife.

"It would be a nice gesture," she agreed. "But really, we're not that popular, and then there is the barrier of language and customs."

"I'd like to," one of the more adventurous American wives agreed. "But I've just taken on another club in my already crowded schedule."

Another week went by, and then I went alone to see Sospeter's wife. She was sweet and brown and shy. The tea she served was spiked with cinnamon bark. There were no language or culture barriers as we laughed at her fat little Nehemiah's antics. We gestured and smiled and I came home with seven new words added to my Swahili vocabulary. That was the beginning of one of the most worthwhile friendships I discovered in those three years.

As my teaching and extracurricular schedule tightened it became difficult to find relaxed time for visiting in the homes of African women. But I could never completely make my peace with the white social whirl which helped to imprison us on our little English island -- the school!

The third year at Livingstone, our Susan was born, and stepping out of the school routine I met Africa a little more head on. The peasants who lived in the villages around our school were a far cry from the students, who dressed like Europeans and would mimic my every utterance with a polite "Yes, ma'am," "No, ma'am," or "Thank you, ma'am!" Walking to a nearby village to buy a chicken, I might pass an old lady.

"Greetings, young one!" she would call. "And what do you carry in your basket?"

"Greetings, old one!" I would reply. "I carry some money."

"Give a poor old woman some money."

"But I must use this money to buy a chicken."

"That is good," she would laugh, gesturing to baby Susan. "Eat well so that you can feed the small one."

"Thank you, old one!"

Two little girls with lengths of bright cloth knotted tightly around their bodies came to our door every morning carrying three beer bottles filled with milk. While I strained the milk into my container they would squat on the verandah, their bright eyes darting in search of any stray pin which might have been swept out of the door with the daily dust. Sometimes older women of the village brought the milk, gesticulating and curious, begging for the empty tin cans which we saved for such occasions, after having discovered the ingenious ways they would be used. Sometimes tin cans served as cups, or they could be cut and beaten into shapes for spoons, knives, or even small kerosine lanterns. At the end of the month the grandfather of the village would arrive to collect his pay for the milk. Always trying to find a chance to use my limited knowledge of Swahili, I welcomed him.

"Good morning, Great One. Was the old lady who brought the milk yesterday your wife?"

"No, that skinny woman was not my wife. My wife is a great big woman," he bragged. "Her breasts hang down to her waist!"

I gulped. That morning I carefully checked out his vocabulary in my dictionary. "That's what he said!" I told Jonathan.

Shortly after this, notice was given that the villagers could only sell their milk to a processing plant in town which was trying to get on its feet. A haughty and sweating young man rode from town every morning with a huge can of milk strapped to the back of his bicycle. He parked a good distance from our house and rang his bell, shouting impatiently, "You are late! Run! Run!" Then he sloshed three dipperfuls of milk into my container.

This arrogant, self-importance frequently characterized those employed in public service. "Hurry! Hurry! Find your seat!" the ticket collector on the local bus would shout, rattling his bag of coins and flourishing the ticket book. But not even a ticket collector could squelch the carnival spirit of the passengers who were determined to enjoy a few hours of holiday until they arrived at their destination. Two men would get into a noisy good-natured argument. A stranger at the back would shout an opinion and soon the whole bus would join in amid loud laughter.

In my pursuit of friendships with African women I discovered that I had to take the initiative. The size of our home, the gadgets we used, the variety of food we dined on, our permanently pressed clothes, and the trips we could personally afford in the school car all spoke of great wealth. Most women were too modest or timid to try to bridge that gap.

An older missionary lady encouraged me to accompany her to a self-help group of local women who met once a week in the school's dining room. Those of us who could sew taught those who could not. The tools were needles, thread, and one small hand-cranked sewing machine. The group of from ten to sixteen women eagerly awaited their turns to try out the machine. As each woman learned a skill she in turn was to pass it on to the women back in her village.

At first, Susan would sleep in her baby carriage, but as she got older she graduated to laps or even swung piggyback style in a brightly colored cloth from the backs of the women who were patiently awaiting their turns at the little sewing machine. To my delight I discovered that they enjoyed my wiry, fine-haired Susan as much as I liked their fat docile babies. Some of the women began to walk home with me for drinks of cold water before following the winding, dusty paths to their own villages.

Sospeter's wife, Mercy, asked me to teach her how to bake bread. Since she did not have the luxury of a gas oven, we experimented at creating an oven by digging a hole in the ground and building a hot wood fire in it. When the fire died out we tucked the loaf pan in the hole and covered it securely with a strip of tin. After lots of practice we managed to balance the temperature correctly. From there we progressed to simple cakes, puddings, and vegetables.

"Now I know why white people don't like their relatives to live with them!" exclaimed Mercy. "Your diet is more expensive than ours and takes more work."

Our friendship developed to the point where halting sentences and smiles and gestures were not enough. "Teach me Swahili," I begged. "Teach me English!" she laughed. Together we slowly learned to communicate, but it was never enough.

Our cultures were strangers and our standards of living were far apart, but I began to discover that as people we were much alike. I learned that an African teacher's wife suffering from a backache and fever enjoyed a cool lotion back rub from a friendly neighbor. An African woman packing to move welcomes a baby-sitter for her lively two-year-old.

One hot forenoon there was a call at the door and I glanced out to see a villager with a few eggs to sell. "I will come," I said and went on preparing for the noon meal. Susan cried and in my busyness the woman was left standing at the door for some minutes. Finally, I tested the eggs in a pan of water and hurriedly paid her. Her face was closed and tired.

A week later I dashed to a white teacher's home to borrow some sugar for our noon meal. "I hear you," a voice responded to my call. I stood with the sun beating on my head. Now I was worried because Susan would be cross with hunger and fatigue and Jonathan wanted to leave early for school. Finally, the door opened.

"I'm so sorry!" apologized the lady of the house. "I thought you were an African calling."

My head throbbed, and as I walked home, my heart hurt a little too. Slowly I was learning.

We were soundly advised by the other staff members to invite a house-servant into our home.

"It will give you more practice in using Swahili," they said.

"There is this fine young man who needs the

pay so that he can go back to school next year."

"A middle-aged widow and her four children are on the brink of starvation. It's a moral obligation to give her a job."

"It's an excellent opportunity to be a witness," counseled one missionary. The same woman warned me to keep my servant in his place. "Lock your cupboards and don't become too chatty. After all, most of the people around here are really heathen! Catholics and Muslims and what have you!"

The students and members of the African community also pressured.

"I will take care of your garden, Madam."

"I have a letter recommending me as a cook."

"I am a serious, trustworthy man who can do clean fast work."

We smiled and shook our heads. "Bado! Bado! Not yet! Not yet!"

As a newly married couple we were still intoxicated with our freedom to shut the door against the world and have a whole house to roam in. And as we got acclimated to our new environment we wanted our home to be a place without an audience. Besides, our home was quite modern with electricity and water-on-the-tap from a lake. In the mornings, to provide us with a supply of hot water, Jonathan would build a wood fire under the boiler while I prepared breakfast. Sometimes Jonathan created more smoke than fire, but in that event we could always heat kettles of water on the stove as we needed it. One trip to the school's tank of rainwater with our bright red plastic bucket provided us with enough drinking water to last two days. On Saturdays Jonathan would fill the tubs with hot water, plug in the electric washing machine, and then take off to do the weekly bargaining for fresh vegetables and fruits in the town's market, while I juggled the cleaning and laundry. Self-reliance was great fun.

Then we had an attack of dysentery and became listless. And by this time we were beginning to loathe our plain diet of tough beef and stringy hamburger. But we had neither the time to go bargaining for a fat hen nor the inner stamina to chop off its head.

That was the week we noticed an increase in the cockroach population.

"They come in under the doors at night and hide their eggs in every little cranny," our neighbor explained, looking around our loose-jointed house. "Give the place a periodic dousing with DDT and that will inhibit them a bit."

Late at night we heard a scratching in the hollow, paneled bedroom door. We flipped on the light in time to watch dozens of giant cockroaches tumble out of the keyhole and scuttle off into the darkness. I dived under the mosquito net while Jonathan bravely squashed them with his slipper.

"Horrible! Horrible!" I wailed.

We ordered DDT and crept listlessly through the school week.

Then for the third consecutive Saturday the school's

water was turned off while the experts mended a break in the pipeline. By noon the water was flowing but now the electric current was turned off to iron out a technical kink in the wiring somewhere. That afternoon as we were wringing out heavy towels and sheets by hand we decided to hire Grace, the widow with four children, for three mornings a week.

Grace was ample and motherly. "You have been married two years and still have no children!" she exclaimed with shocked incredulity. "Do not grieve! Do not despair! Surely God will have mercy and bless you yet."

Grace's prayers must have won out over TAP's austere budget because Susan was born the beginning of our third year in Africa.

Giving birth to a baby in Africa turned out to be a lovely vacation for me. Two weeks before Susan was born I was carefully driven over the corrugated dirt road to town and from there I was flown to the capital city. The next two weeks I read books, knitted, shopped, and sunned myself at a guest house which had an excellent reputation for good food. I missed Jonathan, but after all not everyone can have a baby. Susan was born safely and orderly, and after two more weeks I was flown back to our town. Astride a huge foam rubber cushion in the staff car, I made my debut with Susan onto the school campus. It was nice. As one missionary wife confided to me, "If I could have a baby every couple of years I think I could survive Africa."

When Susan was two months old, Grace asked

off from work to attend the funeral of her half sister, a healthy country girl who at my age had died giving birth to her fifth child. The tipsy night nurse at the government hospital in town had not been able to cope with the complicated delivery. I held Susan close and breathed a very humble prayer.

I liked Grace but our methods of housekeeping conflicted considerably. How to correct someone who was older and far more mature than I was a problem for me.

"In our country it is the custom to dust this way," I would explain, carefully polishing a chair.

Grace stopped slapping the furniture with her cloth and laughed, but she good naturedly tried to indulge my whims.

Susan became another source of conflict. "Feed her! Feed her!" Grace would cry every time the baby whimpered.

Neither could she understand why Susan spent so much time in her crib. "She should be kept close to your body," Grace would admonish. "Tie her to your back."

Truly Susan loved Grace's wide back and swinging motions. I was either too skinny or too tense, for carrying the baby slung to my back never seemed to work well for me, or the baby.

Some motherly soul at the school made out an eating schedule for the expatriate bachelors. When I quit teaching, I was also assigned to the schedule which made me responsible every fourth week for their midmorning tea and noon meal.

"These are huge men with the biggest appetites on the whole campus!" I was warned.

Some of the older staff wives who had cooked for years, seemed to do so with thrift and ease, and turned out marvelous cuisine. My cooking skill was sort of an afterthought and without aid of cake mixes, mushroom sauces, and frozen peas, I was in a panic.

In the States, Mary Emma Showalter's **Mennonite Community Cookbook** had been merely a decorative piece in my kitchen library, but now I claimed it in desperation. I learned that with my wooden paddle I could stir up cakes, cookies and ice cream, stews and dumplings, and I began to have a healthy regard for those quaint, sturdy Mennonite grandmas of bygone years who are so picturesquely illustrated in this cookbook.

The bachelors were a charming lot. A fundamentalistic Bob Jones graduate and a liberal Quaker; a high church Anglican and a low church Anglican. Jonathan and I looked forward to those spicy noontime exchanges with relish.

Any special occasion at the school was marked by a staff supper or tea. There were frequent farewell teas or welcoming teas. Birthdays among the staff were honored by more teas. We staff wives supplied the cakes, cookies, or pies. Always an interesting smorgasbord of American and European pastries was accented by African **mandazies.**

Since Livingstone was a boarding school, and situated four miles from town, a small school shop was maintained for the students. Teachers and subordinate staff members also used it, and non-teaching wives took turns playing shopkeeper each evening after classes.

The shelves in the small room contained no luxuries, only the barest essentials for student or teacher life: bars of harsh blue soap, hard lemon-flavored sweets, sugar, notebooks, paperback New Testaments, tins of plum jam and corned beef and vegetables, a few packs of gelatine dessert, razor blades, and pencils. This was one of the more informal ways I could meet with the students and I was prepared to enjoy it.

My loud friendly American "Hi's!" were a bit too startling I discovered and they watched with cautious amusement as I labored to understand their national currency. Some of our verbal exchanges had a strong creative give and take, but I missed the relaxed wit that one finds so quickly among American students. And no wonder, as English was their memorized language. But they did amazingly well with their stilted, correct, "Yes, ma'am. No, ma'am! Thank you, ma'am. Good evening, ma'am!"

The role of a teacher's wife was to be helpful and I learned to contribute lavishly to the teas and took my turn at dining the school's guests and providing for their lodging. On one occasion I over-did myself. The school's medical dresser had an internal problem which needed urgent repair and I was called upon to dispense the medicines for a month.

In the dispensary, I gazed at the rows of bottles with their long weird medical names and no labels in layman's language.

"But what are they!" I gasped.

"It is no matter, you will soon learn," groaned the dresser.

"Does the chap expect me to give medicine from one bottle at a time till someone dies!" I furiously demanded of Jonathan.

Carefully taking stock, I discovered yeast pills, aspirin, and liniment among all the ominous bottles. Every day the line of students seemed to get longer and soon I had to reorder a giant bottle of yeast pills. I had no idea what value they had, though Jonathan was sure they contained an aphrodisiac drug.

"This will make your blood red," I said without much conviction the first week. The second week I was still giving out yeast pills but singing their praises more forcefully.

Then I found a genuine nurse and with her careful help and documentation, a few more bottles of medicine were put into use. It was an experience which caught me somewhere between a howl and a cry, for it was so unbelievably absurd.

Sometimes I felt the arm of the school was entirely too long, entangling us even in our most private moments. As though any independent action was somehow suspected or written off as unworthy. I gladly contributed to the school but I wanted my private freedom as well, particularly when I stopped teaching to care for our child.

"What are your plans for this morning?" quizzed

a school mother early one morning as I was hanging out a row of diapers on the wash line.

"As soon as I am done here I'll be baby-sitting for the two-year-old of an African friend while she goes to town."

"Oooh . . . I was going to ask you to clean the guest quarters for the bishop who will be staying with the school this weekend."

So instead of baby-sitting, I cleaned.

On another matter I said, "No!"

The staff regularly got their eggs from a small chicken farm close to the school. It was a lovely arrangement as each person could buy according to his needs. Once in a while the chicken farm would run out of feed for a couple of weeks and then we would have to rely on the women who occasionally walked through the school from their villages.

On one particular morning the headmaster's wife found me sitting under a shade tree with Susan, watching a tiny stream of ants drag a beetle to their anthill.

"I have a wonderful idea," she exclaimed. "From now on all the eggs from the egg farm will be brought to your house once a week. You can divide them out, according to orders, peddle them to our homes, and of course, do the bookkeeping for the finances."

For one fleeting minute I thought I was being punished and then I said, "No. Thank you! I simply cannot do that."

"It would have taken every moment of my

freedom," I cried to Jonathan later. "Imagine, coming all the way to Africa to peddle eggs to white people!"

There were times of despair or great joy when I needed a combination of mother-father-confessor. I found this rarity in Elsie, a single missionary who was nearing retirement.

During staff meeting she might mend one of her size forty petticoats so as not to waste time. When the staff's car was not available she spent two days on a local bus accompanying the anemic wife of our school's cook to a mission hospital some distance away. When she greeted a colleague she looked into his eyes and said it with all her heart. She prayed a lot about all those little details which I had been used to taking care of myself. On one occasion I helped her hunt for her house keys which she had lost.

"Elsie, how could you be so careless," she scolded herself. "Oh, Lord, help me to remember where I laid them. Evelyn, I just praise the Lord that He keeps on loving me even though I am so old and forgetful. Oh Lord...."

"It was so confusing," I told Jonathan, "I kept answering during the Lord's turn."

Although Elsie was literally burning out on the mission field she was greatly heartened and challenged by us younger naive TAP-ers who were giving only three years to an overseas country. She not only asked for our ideas but even used them. With Elsie I was free to spill my secret joys and rages at a moment's notice.

Her rebukes were tempered with love and I could even challenge her! It was a freedom of church and fellowship and growth which I had never sampled before.

So it was. The expected and the unexpected; the ridiculous and the solemn; the lovely and the ugly. A time of stretching mentally and spiritually and a time of discovering cavernous voids. To be a TAP wife in Africa was neither all bliss nor all horror. It was, for the most part, I suppose, much like life anywhere: working and eating and having babies and serving tea and going to bed and getting up in the morning and mislaying the scissors and wondering if one would get anything good in the mail this week.

7. VILLAGE AFRICA:

Security and Monotony

We struck out for Ngombe early evening when the sun was no longer a throbbing glare but had slid down the glazed bowl of sky to a more comfortable angle. The round green hills shone in the clear light and the first tints of evening purple lay among the folds of the distant mountains. Aside from the morning hours it was the best time of the equatorial day to be driving. The first hours following an afternoon siesta were hours of promise. And to be traveling to a bush village was an additional promise of venture.

Ngombe was Sospeter's village, "About fifty miles as the crow flies," he had said, trying out another English idiom for style and thrusting vaguely in a northeasterly direction with his chin, a gesture common to the people of his region. Now fifty miles is not an impossible distance for an early evening's drive in Africa -- except for two things: Ngombe was a bush village far from the main road which passed our school lane and led to town. No one I spoke with around the school or mission had ever driven to Ngombe and hence could not tell me the condition of the roads.

"Probably just a path, the last stretch out through there," a veteran missionary put in.

Also, I had learned in my two years in Africa

that asking these people to estimate distance in mileage was opening oneself to some risky surprises. Ask any of the first-year students at Livingstone -- before they had walked it every week -- how far the school lay from town and they would say:

"A mile, sir."

"More like seven, I should think, sir."

"It's three, Mr. Hiebert. Definitely so."

It was actually four.

Of the six nationals on the staff at Livingstone Teachers College, Sospeter was God's gift to me, an answer to my prayers for some African with whom I could begin to build a closer friendship. Perhaps it was because we had something in common -- at least in nature -- that we were attracted to each other. He was quiet, withdrawing from large noisy clusters in the staff room, smiling easily if not a bit nervously; he was eager to please, though not servile in his demeanor of gesture. I was all that, except for one thing.

For all his large brown muscular body Sospeter was a nimble-footed soccer player. Football, they call the game in sub-Sahara Africa. And he played with abandonment, swirling and thrusting his legs and torso more like a ballet dancer than a footballer, until suddenly a foul or rest was called and then Sospeter would break into a great white-toothed laugh, throwing back his head for a moment of disbelief before looking about the field at his fellow players and opponents with an air of detachment, as though somehow never quite believing that he had allowed himself to burst out of his shell again over such a silly matter as a game of sport.

I was a miserable soccer player, though I could play a fair game of basketball. It was Sospeter who worked with me to build a basketball program at Livingstone. At first the boys showed little interest in the game, for basketball, like baseball, while a national sport to Americans, was little known and less understood by the Africans. But through the venture, Sospeter and I reached a mutual appreciation of each other from which sprang a relaxed relationship of candor and trust. A relationship, which I was later to see as peculiar to us -- there was a gulf between many of the nationals and Europeans on the staff. I say humbly that is why Sospeter was a gift from God and an answer to prayers.

We jounced along in the school's stiff-backed Land-Rover truck borrowed for the drive -- Sospeter, Evelyn, and I. The tarmac road ending at Kifutu crossroads a few miles beyond the school, our vehicle now whipped up a halo of red dust. A handful of schoolboys who lived out toward Ngombe hunched together on wooden plank seats on the back of the truck, caged behind heavy wire sides and a canvas top. Along with the students' wooden-box suitcases and our canvas sleeping cots, Sospeter had thrown on a bag of black beans for his mother and a small sack of sugar.

"Few Europeans have visited my village," Sospeter volunteered above the grind of the motor.

"But it's quite a nice little village with papaya trees and the small river nearby."

"It must be fairly small and isolated; I couldn't find it on the Shell Petrol road map," I said.

"True, true. It's very far back in the bush, and the road doesn't go anywhere beyond my village. Years ago an occasional carload or two of Europeans passed through on a hunting safari out into the plains. But now they don't even come."

"What's your village like?" my wife asked. "Something like these we're passing through now?"

"Oh, no! Mine is very clean! These villages along the main roads are very dusty, and many strange people stop in them overnight. They are bad places," Sospeter replied with spark. "And mine is much smaller. About twenty or twenty-five houses and a shop or two. But you will like it; it is very quiet and restful."

We left the main road at the next village, stopping to let off the first schoolboys before turning down a path worn through the bush barely wide enough to admit the Land-Rover. The thorn scrubs reached out to scratch the truck and snag at our clothes through the open windows. Later we would suddenly break out into a large primeval meadow of coarse dry grass with a scattering of mottled humped cattle and the boy herder, standing like a strange black potbellied bird on reed legs; the stick in his hand like a long bill feeding among the grass. We waved and the bird-boy statue burst alive, jumping and swinging his herder's stick above his head. A loin cloth flapped about

his legs.

We passed a few mud-and-wattle huts whose shuttered windows stared back blindly from under the shaggy edge of a grass roof slid askew with age. And then we squeezed into the bush again.

As we pounded along, the confines of the truck cab established a world conducive for developing a deeper affinity with Sospeter. The talk turned to the differences between African and American cultures as expressed in the family relationships.

"You know, Sospeter, what I first observed about African homelife did not jibe with what I had always heard and read."

"How do you mean?"

"Well, as far as I could observe nothing very intimate ever transpired between husband and wife or parents and children. Yet the books wrote endlessly about the tremendous solidarity of the African family, how it ought to be retained, and how Westerners could learn a lesson from it all."

Sospeter broke into laughter.

"But the longer I watched you Africans, I saw how imaginative and complex were your efforts to keep the family laced together."

"You must always remember that the African family is more than just the father and mother and the children," Sospeter put in. "When we think of family we also include uncles and aunts, the grandparents, cousins. Then there may be a second or third wife, each with all her children. As for child-rearing, every adult in the family then is his father or mother. In fact, children often spend a few years living with their uncles or aunts or older brothers and sister."

"It's that child-swapping I fail to understand or appreciate," Evelyn said with conviction. "Why, we knew a Congolese couple studying at the college where we were who had been in the States five years. They had three children which they left behind with grandparents. Two of the children were even preschoolers. At that age I'd want my children to be with me. Not only do they need a mother's affection but they should be under the influence of their parents."

Sospeter shook his head knowingly but did not offer a further comment. He gazed out the window at the passing bush.

"Therein I suppose lies all the difference between us," I said gently, meaning to arbitrate between my wife's maternal instinct and Sospeter's typical African attitude toward their offspring. "The African child is less emotionally tied to his parents than is the American child, but more intimately enmeshed with the extended family than the American."

"We never take our family life for granted," Sospeter volunteered. "It is a difficult tradition to maintain. Not only is there what you call child-swapping, but we travel great distances for visits and hold lengthy palavers to seek counsel and arrive at a consensus, and write letters and send word-of-mouth greetings and messages with friends and travelers passing through our villages. It is like an intricate lesson in geometry, to understand our African family life."

As we rode along in silence for some miles, I recalled an experience of last school term. I drove a truckload of boys from our school to a sports event in the regional capital. They were the football team, my scrubby basketball team, a runner or two, and a few other odd chaps. Nearly a dozen of the players had members of their extended families living in nearby villages. It was one of my first occasions -- and certainly the best -- to observe what transpired between these Teachers College boys and their families in their villages.

As listlessly as the basketball team played, I had the distinct feeling that the fellows were more concerned with seeking out the member or two of their families and reestablishing contact, than they were about whether they won or lost the game. Yet, like I told Sospeter, as far as I could observe when joining some of the fellows on their village visit, nothing very intimate was expressed. At the time I thought it might have something to do with my presence, that any warm display of affection or concern is immediately thwarted before a stranger, and particularly so extrinsic a stranger as a white man.

Mother or auntie was pleased simply that her child came back to the village, and often we would eat alone since we arrived late. Then he would carry a few sticks of wood for the fire or maybe even a tin or two of water -- definitely a woman's job -- to show his mother that he cared for her. Later around a fire he would sit with his brother or uncle, listening to their wisdom and the history of their people. For a few hours the student at a Westernly modeled school again became a villager as that profound African stillness settled down with the darkness closing in. For a few hours the stress of being shaped for a new day in Africa could be escaped by letting the ancient word of the elders fold over him. Everything was at peace again; the youth had returned to his village; the circle was complete. Yet, after a few hours, the student would rise from the elders around the fire gone down and shake off the thick village euphoria to go back gladly to the Teachers College, and to his studies which dug ever wider the chasm separating him from his past.

Outside, night had fallen and the truck lights shot along the narrow tunnel under the low trees and splashed rays upward into the thick black leaves as the truck jounced over potholes and washouts in the road. It was hardly a road anymore -- from the fork a few miles back, where the last of the schoolboys were released, and where Sospeter pronounced that we had only five miles to our destination, his village, Ngombe.

"We're here!" Sospeter's cry broke the silence in the cab later. And at first it seemed that he was playing some joke on us, for ahead lay only the road empty with darkness and the ubiquitous thornbush. But in another minute, even before Evelyn or I could ask Sospeter where his mysterious village lay, suddenly the path flared out to a grassy boulevard and our lights picked up the squat shape of grasshouses and square-walled shops huddled together as if in sleep, so quiet they sat. Except for the dogs, ugly and skinny, which ran into the path of the truck, and yapped hysterically.

I eased the truck into the village, the truck lights pushing back a semicircle of people gathered by the front of the whitewashed shop with its Fanta orange drink and Brook Bond tea signs.

Somehow Sospeter had notified his people that he was bringing some friends home with him for a visit. I never asked him, for I did not wish to shame him, but I imagined that it was a word-of-mouth message carried to them, for I assumed that they were illiterate and thus could not have read a letter. The government's postal service did not extend that far into the bush, and probably wouldn't for another decade.

As we clamored down stiffly from the truck, a woman cried out a greeting to Sospeter and broke from the semicircle of watchers. She wore a wraparound dress of bright green knotted at the shoulder. An oblong head set on a long neck had the hair so closely cropped that at first it appeared shaven. Sospeter introduced her to us as his mother.

Evelyn and I were touched by the extreme politeness of Sospeter's mother, as well as the other older women. On greeting us, they would genuflect on one knee and avert their eyes as they laid a hand limply into ours. Sospeter was undoubtedly correct when he said that few Europeans passed through his village anymore. Indeed, we must have been the first white people in years to have actually stopped in the village. None had ever slept there.

"My mother says that they are wondering just how you two white people are going to get along in our village," Sospeter said to us in English, as we moved from the truck toward a small cluster of people. "I told them that you would eat what they eat and sleep as they sleep," he laughed. "That has marveled them!"

Our eyes grew accustomed to the dim glow from the Land-Rover's amber parking lights and a flickering shallow pool from a lantern falling through an open doorway. The slice of new moon threw down its feeble gleam. Even with that bit of light I could see the group's eyes wide with incredulity, and from some old man came those strange little grunts of surprise the African makes, acclaiming his amazement.

We walked to Sospeter's house, which was really a kind of compound of two small rectangular houses and another tiny grass-roofed circular hut, all of which were partially enclosed by some woven grass mats hanging from a line and a stunted orange tree. On the way to the house Sospeter introduced us to his many brothers and one sister of twelve years. Since the mother was a widow; the chief looked after the girl's welfare; she in turn worked for him.

"Is she in school?" Evelyn asked.

"No. But she is learning to read at home," Sos-

132

peter replied.

"But who is there here to teach her?"

"A few of the people here can read," Sospeter said, a shade of annoyance creeping into his voice. "And I help her when I am home."

"Might she someday be able to attend school?" Evelyn asked.

"I am having difficulties finding enough money for school fees for my brothers. A girl student in the family would be too great a burden."

Supper that night was a chicken, killed in honor of Sospeter's homecoming -- possibly because of us white visitors -- a staple stiff mush called **ugali,** bananas, tea, and cakes. During the meal there was little talk, the food eaten almost hurriedly, until the second glass of tea, which was lingered over.

Sospeter's brothers, who did not eat with us, sat on their haunches some modest distance away. With the food cleared away, they began to ask questions of me. Little by little the family moved closer, and other adults from the village, who could hear that we were now talking and not eating emerged from the darkness and stood about the perimeter of light from the fire. They too asked questions. Sleepy children would stumble in from their play and squeeze up against their ample mothers and stare at us strange white people through the dim firelight.

As my wife asked Sospeter's mother about the health of her children and the size of the gardens she had planted for this season, I looked about the group and felt a bit of that encircling comfort of the village which reaches out to follow its members, whether students, businessmen, or vagabonds, so that they can never forget that center of gravity of acceptance and quiet. Though later years they learn the adventures of big cities and taste the fruits of education and technology, and though they may never again return to live in the boring village, from the village the spirit of the African receives nourishment; there the soul retreats in times of anxiety.

In Sospeter's village I remembered the words of a friend, a fellow colleague teaching in East Africa:

"I often compare African students and their problems with those in North America, with the generation gap and disaffection that seems to be a chronic condition of American society. Here students too feel acutely a generation gap: they despise the fact that their uncles have picked wives for them, that old folks have no idea about what goes on in school, and living for long in an isolated village is impossibly monotonous for them.

"But one difference exists between the African and American youth: none of these young people really wants to be financially or spiritually independent of his family. They all accept the fact that after graduation they will have to pay out half of their salaries for years to come in order that the younger members of the family can go to school as they have.

"Their need for spiritual security shows itself in more conservative ways. Here a student can perhaps doubt the existence of God in philosophy class and call his folks 'primitive' or 'pagan' but when they linger to talk, or hang around a fire at night, they admit that 'the ancestors are wiser than we are,' and regrets are expressed: 'We have lost our traditions and no one can bring them back to us.' God is still up there and the ancestors are still watching."

Evelyn and I came to Ngombe fully expecting to sleep on our cots, but she was given a single bed in a small room of the mother's house.

"Will you join me on a mattress outside for the night?" Sospeter asked me hesitantly.

"Of course," I said eagerly. "Whatever you've arranged is most satisfactory."

"Mrs. Hiebert will sleep in the house with my mother and sister." And then, as if as an afterthought, Sospeter added as he thrust his chin into the darkness behind us, "My brothers sleep over there in that other small house."

And as I lay in the darkness beside Sospeter on some large strangely proportioned cotton mattress thrown on several ground mats, a feeling of satisfaction ran through me. A feeling strong enough to suppress any fears of snakes, hyenas, or thieves. Sospeter knew something of the standard of living we Europeans are accustomed to, yet he trusted in the strength of our mutual friendship to offer the humble facilities of his village home, trusting that we would not despise the offer.

Since coming to East Africa, Evelyn and I have wrestled continuously with the problem of how to bridge the gap of affluence. Often we had occasion to say that God has created all men -- the Asians, Africans, and Europeans -- alike, that we share the same blood. Yet every time I gave witness to that truth, I somehow felt that I heard the clanging of a distant cymbal strike up. Here in one weekend visit to Sospeter's village, we were finally able to give flesh to that word. Yes, in some sense, it was again the word becoming flesh, in dwelling among them. Without saying anything further we were able to let it be known that we did not despise their houses, their food, or their customs. But mostly, that we did not despise them as a technologically less-developed people.

With such thoughts one yawns and smiles and looks up with thanksgiving to the endless acres of bright stars stretched out above him and lets the thick silent African night fold over him in dreams.

Before sleep came, Sospeter talked about many unique things of his tribe, including the native "doctors" or witch doctors as they are more commonly referred to by people from the outside -- individuals who have the power to activate the spirit world for his people. He told of incident after incident of people's lives who were blessed or crippled by these "doctors." Until finally, in further confidence, he testified to the reality of the spirit world in his own past and present life. I found it of interest that Sospeter did not hesitate at all in sharing this totally non-Western phenomenon with a European.

I was not troubled by Sospeter, a Christian, discussing matter-of-factly his belief in an active spirit world operative on his own. I was never able to dismiss the existence of evil spirits, for it seems to me that if we Christians try to teach as Christian doctrine the existence of the Holy Spirit, that ultimate of good spirits, then we have also to accept their beliefs in the existence of evil spirits. To dismiss them is the first step to dismissing the Good Spirit. Superstitions and belief in magic is, of course, a different matter.

Sunday morning we packed the Land-Rover with Sospeter's family and a few old men to drive twelve miles further to another village which boasted a set of mission buildings, a whitewashed church, and an elementary school erected under a stand of mimosa trees, now in their full powdery bloom.

The elder of the church met us, nodding and bobbing and saying yes, yes, very good, very good, and how delighted he was to have us visit his little church and that very soon, very soon, the pastor of the district would arrive on the morning bus. He wore a white shirt, old, yet clean, but it had a hole in it right above the beltline and barely a half inch from his navel. He wore rubber thongs which slapped the pink soles of his feet as he walked; a thin gray jacket, too small to be zippered, flapped about him.

He introduced us to his three sons and wife and showed us his house of mud floors, mud walls, and tin roof. There was no glass in the window openings, only a crude shutter to lock at night.

And I could see that they were very poor and marveled that they continued to serve the church.

The pastor, who had once visited the United States and Canada, arrived on the late bus, carrying a great black Bible wrapped in several protective layers of creased plastic. He sported a long black clip-on tie with an American cowboy horseshoe tiepin. It was past ten o'clock, the scheduled hour for divine worship, but he wanted a few minutes alone with the candidates for baptism, before proceeding with the service. Two smaller bush churches joined this larger village church for today's Sunday service; each had a handful of catechumens to be baptized.

About two hundred people were present, including the children. I was offered a chair on the platform with the elders, since I was a guest, and Sospeter joined me there, since he had brought the guest, and he was home from school and it was not even the holidays. Evelyn stuck by Sospeter's mother and sister, sitting with them on the women's half of the church.

The pastor was eager to introduce his visitors, and I felt that he used me as a white man to gain a few points for himself in the eyes of his flock. He had been to my country, he reminded the people, and knew what an astonishing place America was, and only he could understand fully the great sacrifice I had made in coming to teach in Africa, where I was not getting paid anything; that I had been teaching in Africa for nearly ten years, and the audience was not to be put off by my age, for while I was indeed young, I had something between the eyes! Then he preached about baptism and water and communion and sacrifice and the precious blood flowing down from Calvary.

We all filed out of the church for the baptism service. The pastor lined the seventeen men, women, and children up into two rows and made them kneel and heard their mumbled vows under the thrust of his finger, singling them out one at a time. Then with the elder holding a large blue basin, its porcelain badly chipped, and the water an unholy brown, the pastor taking great handfuls of water doused the believers once for the Father and once for the Son and a third handful for the Holy Spirit, all the while intoning in a large voice the words of the ritual.

There was something festive about the occasion, not at all like the deathly solemnity on the occasion of my own baptism. I looked about me during the baptism service and saw a man, going along the road with a black bull on the end of his rope, stopping to watch the performance. Other passersby paused to watch too. When we all filed back into the church I looked at the new believers sitting with shiny wet heads in the front chairs and thought that now I am one with them in Christ, wondered if they knew that, and wondered too just what that meant.

The Sunday offering was next in the order of service. Each church was to give to its own, since there was very careful reckoning of church monies, the pastor getting his several churches to compete against each other for the year. To keep the money straight, the pastor asked the two visiting bush churches to go outside to take their collection, the one gathering on the east side of the building, the other on the west. Members of the village church remained inside for their offering. So once again people filed out of the church, gathering around their respective elder to give their offering. Then the elders reported the amount to the schoolteacher who was writing on a blackboard the names of the churches and the amount they had given. There was a lengthy delay and some earnest discussion going on in that corner, but I was not understanding it all, until Sospeter began explaining.

It seems that the teacher had bought a goat the night before which was killed and being stewed even now, getting ready for a big dinner after the church service. He had paid forty shillings (about $6.00) and was saying that the goat was his offering. The other churches were upset by this because it put his church's offering way ahead of the others. It took some time until they came to accept the goat as part of the offering, though I was sure that not everyone agreed that it was indeed a forty-shilling goat.

Then it was time for communion. For some reason that I could not uncover with a few guarded questions, there was no bread. Instead, the pastor had brought along a box of plain, sweet biscuits still in their brightly colored package. The biscuits were placed on a flat dish, blessed, and then broken for the communicants. Before they began distributing the sacraments, the pastor told the congregation that any who were unbelievers were to go out of the church and go home, that they were not to hang around outside the doors and windows, and that he would shut the doors and windows but it was too hot.

Sospeter later explained to me that it was their custom to dismiss all unbaptized people from communion so that no one would partake of the holy bread and wine through ignorance or curiosity. With one pastor having oversight of as many as a dozen small churches, and visiting them only once every several months, with the elder being responsible for services on other Sundays, he could not possibly know who were members and who were not.

The communion cup was filled with a strawberry-flavored juice, which tasted suspiciously like a popular local brand of soft drink which had been left sitting open too long and had lost its sparkle of carbonated water. I was curious about this, too, but had the sense not to ask Sospeter about it, much to my wife's relief, she told me later.

During all this, a little baby got restless and whimpered. His mother, unhindered by bra or inhibition, simply took out a slack breast and dropped it into the child's mouth. All this happened while receiving the cup and bread and singing the great Victorian hymns of the church.

Dinner was a feast of **ugali** and goat stew, orange drink, hot tea, and a sweet doughnut-like pastry.

The schoolchildren and older youth amused themselves and their elders with songs and traditional dances which to Western people seem like a kind of loose shuffle accomplished best by disjoining the bones of his body.

Leaving midafternoon to return to Livingstone College was not easy, for farewells, like greetings, can be lengthy occasions for Africans. Everyone came to say good-bye, and many had small gifts for us, apologizing that they had nothing better to offer us since they had not known far enough in advance that we were visiting Sospeter's village.

We were overwhelmed by the gifts and the warmth with which they were given: 23 eggs, a coconut, pineapples, a bag of oranges, a hen, a rooster, an earthenware pot, and a small sculptured piece. We knew of their custom of offering gifts, so we had come prepared with our own to offer Sospeter's family. A new heavy cooking pot, a set of thick drinking glasses, and a piece of cloth for his mother, a large mirror for his sister, and a box of sweets for his younger brothers.

Finally, it was into the Land-Rover cab and down the grassy lane to the wider road leading to Livingstone College, and to another week of teaching. Richer by Ngombe, Sospeter's village.

8. HOLIDAYS:

Retreats and Travel

Shortly after entering the Serengeti National Park we spotted wildebeest by the thousands in their shaggy silvery-gray purple coats, milling in the shade of the acacia. Again at noon, the shadows under the trees made darker by the blue-gray pools of wildebeest. Always the zebra, their circus costumes of contrast subdued with the reddish dust of the veld, their fat matronly rumps flouncing as they ran together with the wildebeest.

At one place a herd of wildebeest flowed across the sandy road in front of our car, jumping a grass-covered gully by the side. It was a sheer symphony of motion and color, the silver-blue wave of manes swelling and falling and breaking to flow out in a long wash of purple pouring under the trees. Later the gazelle, their chestnut and white clean in the open sun, the little Tommies flicking, flicking, nervous and alert. Then a few giraffes, quiet and graceful and demure, looking down with delicate faces and bedroom eyes.

The Serengeti plains were much emptier than I had read them to be, which was attributable to the time of the year, it being the season when the herds of tens of thousands migrated to a far corner of the land on their eternal quest for sweet grass springing up after the rains. When our guide drove us out from the camp through the

143

morning in search for game, we found the buffalo sniffing the wind between munches of dry grass and a few lions at play with their youngsters, but mostly it was the plains wide, stunning, forceful. Even our two-hour afternoon trip yielded less. But I reveled in the ride across the long rise and fall of the land, by the 'waterways of swamps, under the yellow acacias, across the treeless veld, the grass now green, now golden, always shining in the sunlight, and to come again at evenfall, fatigued from the slightly bruising ride, to lie in a hot bath and to eat a hot supper and know that the long, lazy evening of books and letters and conversations would be waiting. Our mind did not return once to Livingstone, neither to the students nor colleagues, nor the work there, for we had slipped into a new world, one without schedules or demands, that strange world of a holiday.

Evelyn and I rode a train to the capital to join Stan and Mary, another TAP couple, for a safari through some African country before taking in the week-long TAP retreat. To prepare one fully for the escape the holiday provided, one needed the horror of the train ride: the four-hour wait on the hot platform Sunday afternoon, the battle to get into the second-class coach to claim the reserved seats, the sweltering, airless waiting inside for another unknown delay, the jubilant feeling when the train first lurched forward, the sudden stopping in the empty bush for the engineers to smite with steel on steel at something in the locomotive's innards, and the infinitely long waiting at stations where the train crew scuffled and drank beer and exchanged good-natured insults with the porters and baggage clerks.

The last part of the ride was uneventful except for the sudden stopping of the train again in the dark desolate bush and the volleys of men's voices bawling from the locomotive, people thrusting the upper halves of their bodies through the open coach windows to learn that a man had fallen off the train into the dust-filled ditch and that we had stopped to pick him up amid curses and protests from the engineers and passengers alike.

We packed the inside and top of Stan's Volkswagen with safari supplies: a tin of petrol, a tin of drinking water, sleeping bags, a wooden box of foodstuffs, and a lantern -- and struck out for the bush, leaving the stink of the train and the mini-traffic snarls of the city behind us. On the road north we always expected to see two or three recent wrecks, and were not disappointed again. They seemed always to involve petrol tankers or other lumbering lorries, and often at a bridge too narrow for both to pass, the larger vehicle assuming the right of way if the smaller one had brakes. On this trip a large truck had turned over and lay like a dead rhino, spilling its entrails of maize and sorghum bags in the dust.

We turned off the main road down a grassy trail with trees sweeping the sides of the car, searching for a picnic spot known only to Stan and Mary, or so they bragged. It was routine to ford the six-inch river, but not five minutes later, as we sat in the shade on the other side, we wondered how we made it. Suddenly the river-bed had swollen to a three-foot torrent, as apparently upcountry somewhere the heat was broken by a flash flood.

We had no plans for staying there for the night, but it would have bordered on suicide to attempt fording now. So we built a fire, ate supper, rolled out the sleeping bags, and sang, "Deep, deep river. . . ." By early light the next morning, when the air was filled with the cries of black and white hornbills and lilac-breasted plovers, we saw that the river had receded to about a foot; we scuttled back to the other side and picked up our road north to the game reserves.

There on the Serengeti plains, open and rolling as an ocean, we spent the night at a lodge, keeping out of the way of a pack of German tourists on one of those quickie packaged tour dips into Africa, all in very proper tourist safari clothes of desert boots, jackets, slacks, sunglasses, and movie cameras.

On the morning we left, I drove the car east along a gravel road through mile after mile of empty savannah, to come at last upon a small hill marked on the map as Lion Hill. Surely there are not many such places like it in the world, for slowly, then more earnestly, the road climbed the hill, curved to ease around the knoll of inselberg, and on that curve we stopped to look back. The land fell away through a golden haze of burnished dry grass, level, yet not level, curving, falling away from our feet where we stood under flat-topped acacias sighing and whispering in the wind. It was a place that refreshed, staggered, diminished, lovely beyond any dreaming of it.

Beyond the park boundary the stone road turned to corrugated ruts, at no speed of which could I get the car to stop the bone-shattering quivering. At one place the car simply left the track and headed into the grass, fortunately level at the side of the road. It rather frightened me and I am sure Stan had an anxious moment too, though he offered no advice. The road was made of small round stones and the VW's hard tires were unyielding, so that at times the car seemed completely to have a mind of its own. Once more before our lunch stop the car again lunged off the road, and I instinctively tried not to whip it back for fear of tipping.

We took lunch in the protection of a dry river-bed, away from a wild wind slamming across the land and drenching down the slopes of wide green hills now growing up about us the farther we traveled. The next miles brought us into even higher hills and long sweeping valleys, the road snaking up, up until we spotted the first cut to look down into Ngorongoro Crater. And who can find a word, a comprehensive word for something so incomprehensible as Ngorongoro? Two thousand feet below, its floor half hidden by wisps of clouds, lay the crater which supports a magnificent collection of African wildlife. We traveled on another dozen miles to an economy resort lodge

Stan had written to for our night's reservations.

When he handed the Indian manager our receipt for reservation, I had a hunch something was wrong. A sullen, troubled look passed over his face, and then he said:

"The people still haven't returned who have the keys to your room."

Then I knew something was amiss, for what hotel doesn't have its people checked out by noon, and there it was three-thirty o'clock, and what manager doesn't have duplicate keys to rooms?

He spent the next half hour in double talk -- saying he has rooms, that he was expecting us, that our rooms were booked double through some oversight at his Arusha office, showing us unfinished quarters, wondering if we'd mind staying there amid the sawdust, wondering if all four of us couldn't stay in one room with three single beds, until finally he said he had one room ready, but it wasn't the one for us. Then he said if the people didn't come for that room by five o'clock, he'd let us have it, saying it as though he were doing us a favor, and as though the paid deposit of our reservation was meaningless.

We ate supper at six and waited another half hour during which Stan and I plotted our final stiff showdown with the chap.

"Look here," we said, "we've waited now for three hours; we'd like to settle into our rooms."

"But I've got only one room," he replied, feigning amazement at our lack of understanding.

"But we have reserved two."

It was a deadlock, and whether he was waiting for us to bribe him to insure our rightful occupancy of the reserved rooms, I do not know, but we decided that since we'd paid for our accommodations, and if he's running a business, then we can be insistent.

Finally, after a long moment, he muttered, "OK, OK. Move in!"

The next morning a solid blanket of mist enveloped the scenery, but we struck out for Ngorongoro Crater anyway, picking up a guide en route. Then it was down the 2,000-foot crater wall over a ragged slash of road and stopping first at a Masai manyatta, a clump of low mud huts, empty, windowless, and in which one couldn't stand up. The guide was very pleased with the desolate village, himself being a Masai, and born in the crater.

Shortly the fog began to lift, and again the animals -- the zebra, the wildebeest, a hippo in a soda lake, a few lions having a "marriage" the guide said -- but of greatest fascination for all of us were the mamma rhino and her overgrown baby. The guide drove straight toward the armored beasts which were trotting off with tails lifted stiffly in the air like wild pigs, overtook them and closed in on their flank. Then they wheeled and charged, the girls screaming and Stan jamming his camera and I thinking the driver was making a monumental mistake by stopping our car and shutting off the engine.

But both the rhino skidded to a stop within five

feet of the car, and stood there snorting and stomping and urinating and looking about with their little pig eyes before turning and running away. The mamma had the very tip of her horn snipped, and wore metal buttons pierced in her ears. When we thawed from our fright and could query the guide's sanity -- he laughing all the while -- we learned from him that he had known these rhino in the crater all his life, and that they will always charge a vehicle but actually never make contact, stopping within a few feet, so he claimed.

Back at the lodge things were going from bad to worse. The Indian manager had taken off for Arusha, perhaps to bawl out those subordinates who double-booked, and had left two African men in charge of preparing the evening meal. To drown their troubles, both had taken too heavy a swig, so that things in the kitchen had reached bedlam proportions. Evelyn and Mary helped rescue the soup and roast amid obsequious blubberings of gratitude from the cooks.

More people arrived without reservations and all of the previous night's guests were staying on so there were no empty beds, and the African sense of hospitality couldn't turn away any clients. They showed a Peace Corps couple to a woodshed where they could lay out their bedrolls, and four Israeli airpilots training a force in Uganda got the lounge floor for the night. It was a thing of joy to watch the Israelis conversing among themselves in Hebrew; they took such open honest delight in each other's presence.

In another two days it was across the plains again to the site of the annual TAP retreat, a great sprawling mission compound in which one could spot an occasional reminiscent whisp of colonial glory; the plant was so large it easily absorbed another three dozen persons for a week's retreat without any appreciable strain.

What do TAP teachers do at an annual retreat? They talk and discuss and sometimes argue and stick up for "their" African country and listen to addresses by national and expatriate "thinkers" and then talk and discuss and argue all over again. And between all that are the games of tennis and croquet, a hike or two, skits, songs, reports, and prayers.

At our annual TAP retreat we had a theme: "Education for Development"; a study book: **A Humanist in Africa,** by Kenneth Kaunda, President of Zambia; and resource persons: Paul M. Miller, an American seminary professor doing a research project; a representative from the Ministry of Education; a representative from the national Christian council; and Donald Jacobs, a Mennonite missionary and TAP director.

What came out of all the talk, prayers, arguments, and communion? On the last night of the retreat a panel of TAP-ers, attempting to assess the conference, came up with four strands which they said ran predominantly through the conference: (1) humanism in Africa, (2) church and state in Africa, (3) the conflict of world views as Western

Christianity comes to traditional Africa, and (4) our concept of Christian service in Africa.

A strong humanitarian emphasis of African governments expresses itself in welfare programs of genuine concern for the less privileged masses. The question immediately arises: What has been the role of the church in this humanitarian emphasis?

There in Africa we were investigating continually the complementary roles of humanism and Christianity. To be sure, the church has been active in humanitarian service, but the idea that Christian thought is compatible with humanistic philosophy reflects the change in contemporary Christian thinking.

Professor Miller claimed that a humanistic outlook was the foundation of the original Anabaptist revival. The new synthesis of Christianity and humanism in Africa may then be a contemporary revival of that revival. However, one has the feeling that the new humanism in Africa is not all that Christian. Miller took issue with some of the reflections in Kaunda's book. The implicit belief in the goodness and perfectibility of man by his own efforts misses both the grandeur and the misery of the biblical portrait of man. Biblical humanism sees both the majesty and the depravity of man. Secular humanism misses both.

Since humanism exalts the dignity of the individual person, does it follow that Western technological society often submerges that individual's interest to expedite mass production? Will traditional humanistic Africa increasingly be depersonalized under the influence of the monolithic forces of modern progress?

A panel of TAP-ers attempted to tangle with these questions. Their thoughts: African society at present still seems to be amenable to a humanistic society though this is changing under the impact of the Western invasion. African society has less pressures, less time schedules, therefore there is more time for people. Technical advance raises living standards but does not necessarily deepen or enrich relationships among people. People are valued for their presence rather than for what they can achieve or produce.

One TAP fellow, in an oral review of Kaunda's book, stated that he felt Kaunda's view of man as potentially capable of achieving perfection by fully realizing his capabilities is too naive and too optimistic.

The African is still basically humanistic in outlook, Kaunda notes, while the Western man has a more impersonal approach to problems, as a result of his living in a technological society. Thus, Africans think differently from Europeans: they tend to **experience** a situation rather than **solve** a problem, and worry little about the differences between the natural and the supernatural.

All this is extremely interesting and relevant for all of us North Americans and Europeans in TAP, attempting to teach African students.

On the subject of church and state relationships in Africa, Donald Jacobs said that sometimes in Africa it is difficult to distinguish between the work of the church and the work of the state.

"The church and state are not so carefully separated here in Africa as they are in North America. In a struggling, less-developed country, the church spends much of her time being involved in problems like how can the people get more food to eat. And the government sometimes asks dedication and sacrifice of the people that exceed what the church requires. All of this forces us to reexamine our traditional ideas of the church and state."

Speaking on socialism and Christianity, another TAP-er said that if the government is a good government and concerned for the welfare of all its citizens, then the church in a less-developed country has an obligation to cooperate with government. However, as the church is working with government for material progress it should mainly emphasize the inner spiritual values which are embedded in the good life.

Thus, though the government is striving, and rightly so, for a certain minimum level of material welfare which is necessary for the good life, the church must reaffirm that the good life consists not only in the material advancement but also in a spiritual quality of living which finds its outward expression in Christlike service. The church needs to reaffirm that honesty, hard work, and efficiency have certain intrinsic rewards in and of themselves. The growth of mature character, the flowering of God-given talents and abilities, the sense of mission, and purpose in one's vocation are ultimately the more rewarding results of ethical living.

As well as cooperating with government, the church has an obligation to stand apart from government. It must reserve the right to dissent if necessary. Perhaps the most significant role of the church is to be a prophetic voice in the land, not so bound to any vested group that its voice is stifled.

In a poor country, TAP-ers should see how they can climb down the socioeconomic ladder to better identify with those they are supposedly "serving." That suggestion brought forth some lively discussion, particularly in light of the fact that the previous day during a business session the TAP director announced that living allowances would increase.

Personally, Stans and we were disappointed to learn of this decision without an objective study of the need for such a raise. We found it additionally upsetting when discussing our opinion with other TAP-ers to hear some of their expressions. It seemed that a few felt that TAP is a kind of profit-sharing program rather than a service program with a maintenance allowance. Some felt that one should be able to save enough money from his allowance to do a grand six-week to two-month tour of Europe en route home. Others felt that owning a personal car in Africa was such a risk they needed some kind of financial cushion in the event of vehicular calamity. One person told of a former TAP couple who lived so frugally they bought a new car with their TAP savings on returning to the States. He related the account as though it were some kind of achievement of budgetary excellence.

The conflict of world views also got a good airing. It is inevitable that Western-oriented TAP teachers, in the midst of a radically different culture, should wrestle with the question of the conflict of world view.

"We shall never understand the African if we do not understand his concept of the 'group' and his relationships within that group," missionary-anthropologist Jacobs related. "Reality for the African is intimately tied up with his group –– all those with whom he has relationships, both living and dead."

Jacobs said that for the African, life's pilgrimage is an exercise in discovering his quality of spirit and increasing this spirit or soul strength through life. Soul strength is enlarged by increasing one's relationships within the group. Thus the African always tends to be communally minded. In fact, the very position he occupies in the after world depends on the strength and number of his relationships acquired in this life.

How does all this affect the African ethic? Because the Bantu world view is so strongly man-centered and governed by human interrelationships, Bantu ethics tend to be highly situational. One can't expect rigid normative ethics since the human situation is always in flux. One can't assume something is eternally right or wrong, since ethical answers come out of the way the group is thinking at the moment.

The African then is an expert in the realm of human relationships. Ethics as he conceives of it must strengthen the group and unify it. This has tremendous relevance in the area of disciplines in the school situation, for instance. Thus, one deals with a person in the context of a group. One deals with a deviant to bring him back into the group. It is not primarily for the individual's benefit, but for the group's.

"In a society itself, the general outlook of the people themselves is usually in a state of flux," Jacobs stated. "It is either a liberal phase of change away from traditional values or in a conservative reaction, where the elements of the traditional past are consciously sought after again.

"The church in Africa was the producer of the original liberal swing away from the traditional culture. Now the question is whether the Christian church here is African enough so that in the contemporary revival of African culture the church can follow this trend and work in this situation."

Naturally, church volunteers should spend a sizable portion of a retreat in considering their concept of service: what is the nature of our service as TAP teachers in Africa? What is our role as "servants" in an African culture? In what way is our service distinctly Christian, if indeed it is?

One crucial question batted around during one discussion period was, Can there be service without sacrifice, service without suffering? It is human to

157

avoid suffering but what if by avoiding suffering our service is hindered or restricted? If service leads us to suffer we ought not to avoid it. However, suffering ought not be an end in itself. Genuine sensitivity to those in real need can lead to suffering for a true servant of Christ. Thus, genuine Christian service will lead to suffering.

In a closing communion service, Jacobs spelled this out in theological terms. We are called to share in Christ's death. This will involve many things and be different for different people. We are called to die to our pet prejudices, to our love of ease and luxury, to the importance of our real and imagined status, to our right to be right. Dying to such treasures as these will not be easy. It will involve suffering.

During a commitment service, a quiet Quakersque meeting with much time for meditation, we contemplated the "why" of our commitment, the many reasons that we had come to East Africa. Most of us would have to admit to a bag of mixed motives. Then we reflected on why we resist commitment and noted that because the things on which we trusted for security were threatened: the old patterns of life, our position among men, our past relationships with others. God would call us away from ephemeral sources of security, offering to us Himself instead. He enlarges our lives in commitment. He takes us out of our small lives and into His great one. As one TAP-er summed it up:

"Without commitment to Christ, we are only ourselves."

Photo by Burton Buller

THE AUTHOR

Born in Hagerstown, Maryland, Omar Eby took his BA degree at Eastern Mennonite College, Harrisonburg, Virginia, and his MA degree at Syracuse University. He has taught for six years in three African countries: Somalia, Tanzania, and Zambia.

In the States he has taught at the high school and college levels, edited a monthly mission magazine, and served as Director of Information Services for the Mennonite Central Committee, Akron, Pennsylvania.

Mr. Eby teaches English and journalism at Eastern Mennonite College, Harrisonburg, Va. He is the author of four other books.